COLLECTED WORKS OF RENÉ GUÉNON

THE CRISIS OF THE MODERN WORLD

RENÉ GUÉNON

THE CRISIS OF THE MODERN WORLD

Translators

Marco Pallis
Arthur Osborne
Richard C. Nicholson

SOPHIA PERENNIS

HILLSDALE NY

Originally published in French as
La Crise du Monde Moderne
© Éditions Gallimard 1946
Fourth, revised edition 2001
(Second Impression 2004)
Third edition, Sophia Perennis, Ghent 1996
Second edition 1962, 1975, Luzac & Company, London
First edition 1942, Luzac and Company, London
English translation © Sophia Perennis 2001

Series editor: James R. Wetmore

For information, address:
Sophia Perennis, P.O. Box 611
Hillsdale NY 12529
sophiaperennis.com

Library of Congress Cataloging-in-Publication Data

Guénon, René
[La crise du monde moderne. English]
The crisis of the modern world / René Guénon ; translated by
Arthur Osborne, Marco Pallis, Richard C. Nicholson

p. cm. — (Collected works of René Guénon)
Includes index.
ISBN 0 900588 24 1 (pbk: alk. paper)
ISBN 0 900588 50 0 (cloth: alk. paper)
1. Culture. 2. Civilization, Modern. 3. Evolution. I. Title
HM621.G8413 2001
306'.094—dc21   2001001094

CONTENTS

EDITORIAL NOTE

THE PAST CENTURY HAS WITNESSED an erosion of earlier cultural values as well as a blurring of the distinctive characteristics of the world's traditional civilizations, giving rise to philosophic and moral relativism, multiculturalism, and dangerous fundamentalist reactions. As early as the 1920s, the French metaphysician René Guénon (1886–1951) had diagnosed these tendencies and presented what he believed to be the only possible reconciliation of the legitimate, although apparently conflicting, demands of outward religious forms, 'exoterisms', with their essential core, 'esoterism'. His works are characterized by a foundational critique of the modern world coupled with a call for intellectual reform; a renewed examination of metaphysics, the traditional sciences, and symbolism, with special reference to the ultimate unanimity of all spiritual traditions; and finally, a call to the work of spiritual realization. Despite their wide influence, translation of Guénon's works into English has so far been piecemeal. The *Sophia Perennis* edition is intended to fill the urgent need to present them in a more authoritative and systematic form. A complete list of Guénon's works, given in the order of their original publication in French, follows this note.

Though first published in 1927, *The Crisis of the Modern World* bears reprinting unaltered and unannotated at the beginning of this new millenium, for it rests upon principles that stand outside—indeed determine—the conditions of time and space. What few particular illustrative points may be 'dated' will be readily identified and put in perspective by those readers for whom Guénon intended the book. In this very important book, which has become a classic, René Guénon analyzes the crisis of our times from the metaphysical point of view. That is, it is diagnosed not as a degradation of morals, which is a perversion of the will, but as the degradation of knowledge, that is, a perversion of the intellect. Such intellectual analysis of present disorders is not merely a legitimate supplement to the moral approach with which we are more familiar: it is fundamentally necessary and it has been carried out in this book with profundity and penetration.Guénon often uses words or expressions set off in 'scare quotes'. To avoid clutter, single quotation marks have been used throughout. As for transliterations, Guénon was more concerned with phonetic fidelity than academic usage. The system adopted here reflects the views of scholars familiar both with the languages and Guénon's writings. Brackets indicate editorial insertions, or, within citations, Guénon's additions. Wherever possible, references have been up-dated, and English editions substituted.

Two previous translations of *The Crisis of the Modern World* were consulted in the preparation of this edition, that of Arthur Osborne, first published in 1942, and that of Marco Pallis and Richard C. Nicholson, which included some revisions and deletions, and first appeared in 1962. The entire text was then restored and checked for accuracy and further revised by William Stoddart. For other assistance thanks go to Benjamin Hardman, Allan Dewar, and John Ahmed Herlihy. A special debt of thanks is owed to Cecil Bethell, who revised and proofread the text at several stages and provided the index. Cover design by Michael Buchino and Gray Henry, based on a drawing of a *chimaera* by Guénon's friend and collaborator Ananda K. Coomaraswamy.

THE WORKS
OF RENÉ GUÉNON

PREFACE

WHEN WRITING *East and West* a few years ago, we thought we had said all that was required, at least for the time being, concerning the questions dealt with in that book. Since then however events have succeeded one another at an ever increasing speed and, while this has not made it necessary to alter a single word of what we wrote at that time, it provides an opportunity for certain additional explanations and for the development of lines of thought that we did not feel called upon to stress in the first instance. These explanations have become all the more necessary because we have recently seen a distinctly aggressive reaffirmation of some of those very confusions we had already tried to dispel. For this reason, while carefully staying aloof from all controversy, it has seemed to us advisable to present matters once more in their true perspective. In this connection there are certain considerations, often of a quite elementary nature, which appear so alien to the vast majority of our contemporaries that in order to make them generally understood it is necessary to return to them again and again, presenting them in their various aspects and explaining more fully, as circumstances permit, any points likely to give rise to difficulties that could not always be foreseen from the outset.

The very title of the present volume calls for some initial explanation, if what it means is to be clearly understood and all misrepresentation prevented. Many no longer doubt the possibility of a world crisis, taking the latter word in its most usual acceptation, and this in itself marks a very noticeable change of outlook: by sheer force of circumstance certain illusions are beginning to vanish, and we cannot but rejoice that this is so, for it is at any rate a favorable symptom and a sign that a readjustment of the contemporary mentality is still possible—a glimmer of light as it were—in the midst of the present chaos. For example, the belief in a never-ending 'progress', which until recently was held as a sort of inviolable and indisputable dogma, is no longer so widespread; there are those who perceive, though in a vague and confused manner, that the civilization of the West may not always go on developing in the same direction, but may some day reach a point where it will stop, or even be plunged in its entirety into some cataclysm. Such persons may not see clearly where the danger lies—the fantastic or puerile fears they sometimes express being proof enough that their minds still harbor many errors—but it is already something that they realize there is a danger, even if it is felt rather than understood; and it is also something that they can conceive that this civilization, with which the moderns are so infatuated, holds no privileged position in the history of the world, and may easily encounter the same fate as has befallen many others that have already disappeared at more or less remote periods, some of them having left traces so slight as to be hardly noticeable, let alone recognizable.

Consequently, when it is said that the modern world is in the throes of a crisis, this is usually taken to mean that it has reached a critical phase, or that a more or less complete transformation is imminent, and that a change of direction must soon ensue—whether voluntarily or no, whether suddenly or gradually, whether catastrophic or otherwise, remaining to be seen. This use of the word 'crisis' is perfectly legitimate, and indeed corresponds in part to what we think ourselves; but in part only, for our point of view is a more general one: for us it is the modern age in its entirety that is in a state of crisis, which is precisely why we entitled this book *The Crisis of the Modern World*. It seems however that the crisis is nearing its solution, and this has the effect of emphasizing still further the abnormality of the state of affairs that has already existed for some centuries, though the consequences were never before so apparent as they are now. This is also the reason for the increasing speed with which events are now unfolding: such a state of affairs may doubtless continue for some time longer, but not indefinitely, and, even without being able to assign a definite time-limit, one has the impression that it cannot last very much longer.

But the word 'crisis' also contains other implications making it an even more apt term for what we wish to express: indeed, its etymology—which is often lost from sight in current usage but must be kept in mind if one wishes to restore to the word its full meaning and original value—makes it to some extent synonymous with the words 'judgement' and 'discrimination'. The phase that can properly be termed 'critical' in any order of things is the one immediately preceding a resolution, be this favorable or unfavorable—in other words, one in which a turn is taken either for the better or for the worse; it is therefore the phase in which it is possible to pass judgement on the results achieved, to balance the pros and the cons, and, to some extent, to classify the results (either positively or negatively) and to see which way the balance will swing in the end. We do not aim, of course, at giving a classification that will be totally complete; to do this would be premature, since the crisis is not yet ended and since it is perhaps impossible even to say exactly when, and in what manner, it will end. It is always preferable to refrain from prognostications that cannot be based on grounds clearly intelligible to all, and that therefore could be misinterpreted, adding to the confusion rather than relieving it. All we can undertake at the moment is to contribute, to a certain extent and as far as the means at our disposal allow, toward making those capable of it aware of some of the consequences that seem already fully established. By so doing we shall be preparing the ground, albeit in a partial and rather indirect manner, for those who must play their part in the future 'judgement', following which a new era will open in the history of mankind.

Certain of the expressions just used will doubtless awaken in the minds of some the idea of what is called the Last Judgement, or Doomsday, and quite correctly, though whether this be understood literally or symbolically or in both ways (since in reality the two conceptions are not mutually exclusive) is here of little consequence; nor is this the place or time for a fuller explanation of this point. In any case, the reference to 'balancing pros and cons' and 'judging results either positively or negatively' may well have suggested the division of the 'chosen' and the 'damned' into two groups to be thus immutably fixed henceforward. Even if this is but an analogy, one must admit that it is valid, well-founded, and in conformity with the nature of things—a point that calls for further explanation.

It is certainly no accident that so many people today are haunted by the idea of the 'end of the world'; it may be regrettable in some respects, since the extravagances to which this idea when ill-understood gives rise, and the messianic vagaries that spring from it in certain circles—all of them manifestations of the mental disequilibrium of our time—only aggravate this same disequilibrium to an extent that is impossible altogether to overlook; nevertheless, this obsession with the 'end of the world' is a fact that one cannot ignore. No doubt the most convenient attitude when confronted with things of this kind is simply to dismiss them without further enquiry as errors or fantasies of no importance; we consider however that even if they are in fact errors, it is better, while denouncing them as such, to probe for the reasons that have given rise to them and to seek the modicum of truth—deformed though it may be—that they may nevertheless contain; for, since error has after all a purely negative manner of existence, absolute error cannot exist anywhere and is indeed a meaningless expression. If the matter is viewed in this way, it becomes easy to see that the preoccupation with the 'end of the world' is closely connected with the state of general mental unrest in which we are at present living: the vague foreboding of an end—which in fact is near—works uncontrollably on the imaginations of some people and quite naturally gives rise to wild and for the most part grossly materialized mental images that in their turn assume external form in the extravagances to which we have alluded. This explanation is however no excuse for such extravagances; at least, even if the persons who fall involuntarily into error, being predisposed to it by a mental state for which they are not responsible, are to be excused, it can never be a reason for excusing the error itself. For our part, we certainly cannot be accused of undue indulgence toward the 'pseudo-religious' manifestations of the contemporary world, any more than toward modern errors in general. Indeed, we know that there are those who would be inclined rather to reproach us with the opposite of tolerance, and it may be that what is said here will enable them to understand better our attitude in these matters, an attitude that consists in abiding always by the only point of view that concerns us—that of impartial and disinterested truth.

But this is not the whole question at issue: a purely psychological explanation of this idea of the 'end of the world' and of its current manifestations, accurate though it may be in its own order, could never be fully adequate; to accept it as such would be to yield to one of those modern illusions which we take every opportunity of condemning. As we have said, there are those who have a vague feeling that something is approaching its end, without being able to define exactly the nature or extent of the change they foresee; it is impossible to deny that this feeling is based on reality, even though it be vague and subject to false interpretations or imaginative deformations, for, whatever may be the nature of the end that is approaching, the crisis that must necessarily lead up to it is apparent enough, and there is no lack of unequivocal and easily perceptible signs all pointing with one accord to the same conclusion. This end is doubtless not the 'end of the world' in the complete sense in which some persons seek to interpret it, but it is at least the end of a world: and if it is Western civilization in its present form that is to end, it is understandable that those who are accustomed to see nothing beyond it, and for whom this is 'civilization' unqualified, should incline to the belief that everything will end with it and that its disappearance will in fact be 'the end of the world'.

It may then be said, in order to reduce the question to its true proportions, that we really do seem to be approaching the end of a world, in other words, the end of an epoch or a historical cycle, which may also correspond to the end of a cosmic cycle, in accordance with the teaching of all traditional doctrines on the subject. There have already been many occurrences of this sort in the past, and there will doubtless be others in the future; these occurrences are of varying importance, according to whether they terminate longer or shorter periods, and whether they affect the whole of mankind or merely one or another of its component parts—that is, some particular race or people. It is to be expected that, in the present state of the world, the impending change will be widespread and that, whatever form it may assume—a point we shall not attempt to determine—it will affect more or less the whole world. In any case, the laws governing such occurrences apply analogously at different levels, so that what is true of the 'end of the world' in the most complete sense in which this can be conceived—it is usually taken to refer only to the terrestrial world—is also true on a proportionately lesser scale of some particular world in a much more restricted sense of the word.

These preliminary remarks should make it easier to understand the questions we are about to consider. We have already had occasion to refer fairly frequently in other works to the 'cyclic laws'; it would be difficult, perhaps, to give a complete exposition of them in a form easily comprehensible to Western minds, but one must at least have a certain amount of data on the subject to appreciate the true nature of the present age and to see its exact place in world history. We shall therefore begin by showing that the characteristic features of this age are in fact those that the traditional doctrines have from all time indicated for the cyclic period to which it corresponds; and in so doing we shall make it clear that what is anomaly and disorder from one point of view is nevertheless a necessary element of a vaster order, and an inevitable consequence of the laws governing the development of all manifestation. Let it be said at once however that this is no reason to submit passively to the disorder and obscurity that seem to be triumphing at the moment, for were it so we should have nothing better to do than to remain silent; on the contrary, it is a reason for striving to the utmost to prepare the way out of this 'dark age', for there are many signs that its end is already relatively near, if not imminent. This also is a part of the appointed order of things, for equilibrium is the result of the simultaneous action of two contrary tendencies; if the one or the other could cease to act entirely, equilibrium would never be restored and the world itself would disappear; but this supposition has no possibility of realization, for the two terms of an opposition have no meaning apart from each other, and whatever the appearances may be, one may be sure that all partial and transitory disequilibriums contribute in the end toward realizing the total equilibrium.

1

THE DARK AGE

THE HINDU DOCTRINE teaches that a human cycle, to which it gives the name *Manvantara*, is divided into four periods marking so many stages during which the primordial spirituality becomes gradually more and more obscured; these are the same periods that the ancient traditions of the West called the Golden, Silver, Bronze, and Iron Ages. We are now in the fourth age, the *Kali-Yuga* or 'dark age', and have been so already, it is said, for more than six thousand years, that is to say since a time far earlier than any known to 'classical' history. Since that time, the truths which were formerly within reach of all have become more and more hidden and inaccessible; those who possess them grow fewer and fewer, and although the treasure of 'nonhuman' (that is, supra-human) wisdom that was prior to all the ages can never be lost, it nevertheless becomes enveloped in more and more impenetrable veils, which hide it from men's sight and make it extremely difficult to discover. This is why we find everywhere, under various symbols, the same theme of something that has been lost—at least to all appearances and as far as the outer world is concerned—and that those who aspire to true knowledge must rediscover; but it is also said that what is thus hidden will become visible again at the end of the cycle, which, because of the continuity binding all things together, will coincide with the beginning of a new cycle.

It will doubtless be asked why cyclic development must proceed in this manner, in a downward direction, from higher to lower, a course that will at once be perceived to be a complete antithesis to the idea of progress as the moderns understand it. The reason is that the development of any manifestation necessarily implies a gradually increasing distance from the principle from which it proceeds; starting from the highest point, it tends necessarily downward, and, as with heavy bodies, the speed of its motion increases continuously until finally it reaches a point at which it is stopped. This fall could be described as a progressive materialization, for the expression of the principle is pure spirituality; we say the expression and not the principle itself, for the latter, being beyond all oppositions, cannot be described by any term appearing to suggest an opposite. Moreover, words such as 'spirit' and 'matter', which we borrow here from Western terminology for the sake of convenience, have for us little more than a symbolical value; in any case, they can be made to fit the question in hand only on condition that we exclude the special interpretations given them by modern philosophy, whose 'spiritualism' and 'materialism' are, in our eyes, only two complementary forms that imply each other and are both negligible for anyone who wishes to go beyond these contingent points of view. However, since it is not of pure metaphysics that we propose to treat here, if all due precautions are taken to avoid ambiguity, and if the essential principles are never lost from sight, we may accept the use of terms that, although inadequate, nevertheless serve to make things more easily understandable, so long, of course, as this can be done without distorting what is to be understood.

What has been said of the development of manifestation gives a picture that is accurate when viewed as a whole, but is nonetheless too simplified and rigid in that it may give the idea of development along a straight line—in one direction only and without oscillations of any sort—whereas the truth is actually far more complex. In point of fact, as we have already said, two contrary tendencies are to be traced in everything, the one descending and the other ascending, or, in other words, one centrifugal and the other centripetal; and, from the predominance of one or the other tendency result two complementary phases of manifestation, the one a departure from the principle and the other a return to it, two phases often symbolically compared to the beating of the heart or the process of breathing. Although these two phases are usually described as successive, the two tendencies to which they correspond must in reality be conceived as always acting simultaneously—although in different proportions—and it sometimes happens, at moments when the downward tendency seems on the point of prevailing definitively in the course of the world's development, that some special action intervenes to strengthen the contrary tendency, and to restore a certain equilibrium, at least relative, such as the conditions of the moment allow; and this causes a partial readjustment through which the fall may seem to be checked or temporarily neutralized.[1]

It is obvious that these traditional data, of which we can give only a bare outline here, open the way to conceptions that are deeper, wider, and altogether different from the various attempts at a 'philosophy of history' that are so popular with modern writers. However, we have for the moment no intention of going back to the origin of the present cycle, or even to the beginning of the *Kali-Yuga*; we shall only be concerned, directly at least, with a far more limited field, namely with the last phases of the *Kali-Yuga*. Actually, within each of the great periods of which we have spoken it is possible to go further, and distinguish secondary phases constituting so many sub-divisions of it, and since each part is analogous after its own fashion to the whole, these subdivisions reproduce, so to speak, on a much smaller scale, the general course of the greater cycle in which they are contained; but here also a complete investigation of the ways in which this law applies to particular cases would carry us beyond the limits of the present study.

We shall conclude these preliminary remarks by mentioning only one or two particularly critical periods among those through which mankind has more recently passed, that is, among those falling within the period usually called 'historical', as it is in fact the only one really accessible to ordinary or 'profane' history; and this will lead us directly to the real object of our study, since the last of these critical periods is none other than the one that constitutes what is termed the modern age.

It is a strange fact, and one which appears never to have received proper attention, that the strictly 'historical' period—in the sense that we have just indicated—goes back exactly to the sixth century before the Christian era, as though there were at that point a barrier in time impossible to penetrate by the methods of investigation at

---

1. This is connected with the function of 'divine preservation', which is represented in the Hindu tradition by Vishnu, and more particularly by the doctrine of *Avatāras* or 'descents' of the divine Principle into the manifested world, a doctrine that we cannot undertake to develop here.

the disposal of ordinary research. Indeed, from this time onward there is everywhere a fairly precise and well-established chronology, whereas for everything that occurred prior to it only very vague approximations are usually obtained, and the dates suggested for the same events often vary by several centuries. This is very noticeable even in the case of countries of whose history we possess more than a few scattered vestiges, such as Egypt, for example; but what is perhaps even more astonishing is that in an exceptional and privileged case like that of China, which possesses annals relating to far more distant periods and dated by means of astronomical observations that leave no room for doubt, modern writers nonetheless class these periods as 'legendary', as if they saw in them a domain in which they have no right to any certainty, and in which they do not allow themselves to obtain any. So-called 'classical' antiquity is therefore a very relative antiquity, and far closer to modern times than to real antiquity, since it does not even go back to the middle of the *Kali-Yuga*, whose length is itself, according to the Hindu doctrine, only a tenth part of the whole *Manvantara*; and this is sufficient indication of how far the moderns are justified in priding themselves on the extent of their historical knowledge. They will doubtless seek to justify themselves by replying that all this refers only to 'legendary' periods and is therefore unworthy of consideration; but this reply in itself is an admission of ignorance and of a lack of comprehension that can be explained only by their contempt for tradition; the specifically modern outlook is in fact, as we shall explain further on, identical with the anti-traditional outlook.

In the sixth century before the Christian era considerable changes took place for one reason or another among almost all peoples, changes which however varied in character from country to country. In some cases it was a readaptation of the tradition to conditions other than those previously prevailing, a readaptation that was accomplished in a rigorously orthodox sense. This is what occurred for example in China, where the doctrine, primitively established as a single whole, was then divided into two clearly distinct parts: Taoism, reserved for an elite and comprising pure metaphysics and the traditional sciences of a properly speculative nature, and Confucianism, which was common to all without distinction, and whose domain was that of practical and mainly social applications. Among the Persians there seems also to have been a readaptation of Maz-daism, for this was the time of the last Zoroaster.[2] In India on the other hand this period saw the rise of Buddhism,[3] that is to say of a revolt against the traditional spirit, amounting to a denial of all authority and resulting in a veritable anarchy, in the etymological sense, of 'absence of principle', both in the intellectual and social realms. It is a curious fact that there are no monuments in India dating from before this period, the orientalists having tried to make this fact tell in favor of their tendency to find the origins of everything in Buddhism, the importance of which they strangely exaggerate. The explanation of the fact is nevertheless quite simple; it is that all earlier constructions were of wood and have therefore left no trace.[4] Such a change in the mode of construction must have corresponded however to a profound modification of the general conditions governing the existence of the people concerned.

Moving westward we see that for the Jews this was the time of the Babylonian captivity and perhaps one of the most astonishing of all these happenings is the fact that a short period of seventy years should have sufficed for the Jews to forget even their alphabet, so

---

2. It should be noted that the name Zoroaster does not really designate any particular person, but a function that is both prophetic and legislative; there were several Zoroasters, who lived at very different periods; it is probable that it was a function of a collective nature, as was that of Vyāsa in India; likewise in ancient Egypt, what was attributed to Thoth or Hermes represented the work of the whole sacerdotal caste.

3. The question of Buddhism is by no means so simple as this brief account of it might suggest; and it is interesting to note that if, as far as their own tradition is concerned, the Hindus have always condemned the Buddhists, this is not the case with the Buddha himself, for whom many of them have a great reverence, some going so far as to see in him the ninth Avatāra. As for Buddhism such as it is known today, one should be careful, in dealing with it, to distinguish between its *Mahāy-āna* and its *Hīnayāna* forms, that is, between the 'Greater' and the 'Lesser' Vehicles; in general one may say that Buddhism outside India differs markedly from the original Indian form, which began to lose ground rapidly after the death of Ashoka and eventually disappeared.

4. This is a state of affairs not peculiar to India, but met with in the West as well; it is for the same reason that no traces remain of the cities of the Gauls, the existence of which is however undeniable, being testified to by contemporary witnesses; and here also modern historians have profited by the lack of monuments to depict the Gauls as savages living in forests.

that afterward the sacred books had to be reconstructed in quite different characters from those in use up to that time. It would be possible to cite many other events belonging more or less to the same date: we will only mention that for Rome it was the beginning of the 'historical' period, which followed on the 'legendary' period of the kings, and it is also known, though somewhat vaguely, that there were important movements among the Celtic peoples at this time; but without elaborating these points we must pass on to consider what happened in Greece. There too, the sixth century was the starting-point of the so-called 'classical' civilization, which alone is entitled—according to the moderns—to be considered 'historical', everything previous to it being so little known as to be treated as 'legendary', even though recent archeological discoveries no longer leave room for doubt that there was a very real civilization; and we have reasons for supposing that this first Hellenic civilization was far more interesting intellectually than what followed, and that the relationship between the two is to some extent analogous to that between medieval and modern Europe. It should be noted however that the breach was not so complete as in the latter case, for at least a partial re-adaptation was carried out in the traditional order, principally in the domain of the 'mysteries'; one may refer here to the case of Pythagorism, which was primarily a restoration, under a new form, of the earlier Orphic tradition, and whose connection with the Delphic cult of the Hyperborean Apollo bears witness to an unbroken and regular line of descent from one of the most ancient traditions of mankind. But on the other hand there very soon appeared something of which there had been no previous example, and which, in the future, was to have an injurious effect on the whole Western world: we refer to that special form of thought that acquired and retained the name of 'philosophy'; and this point is important enough to warrant our dwelling on it at somewhat greater length.

It is true that the word 'philosophy' can, in itself, be understood in quite a legitimate sense, and one which without doubt originally belonged to it, especially if it be true that Pythagoras himself was the first to use it: etymologically it denotes nothing other than 'love of wisdom'; in the first place, therefore, it implies the initial disposition required for the attainment of wisdom, and, by a quite natural extension of this meaning, the quest that is born from this same disposition and that must lead to knowledge. It denotes therefore a preliminary and preparatory stage, a step as it were in the direction of wisdom or a degree corresponding to a lower level of wisdom;[5] the perversion that ensued consisted in taking this transitional stage for an end in itself and in seeking to substitute 'philosophy' for wisdom, a process which implied forgetting or ignoring the true nature of the latter. It was in this way that there arose what may be described as 'profane' philosophy, in other words, a pretended wisdom that was purely human and therefore entirely of the rational order, and that took the place of the true, traditional, supra-rational, and 'non-human' wisdom. However, there still remained something of this true wisdom throughout the whole of antiquity, as is proven primarily by the persistence of the 'mysteries', whose essentially initiatic character is beyond dispute; and it is also true that the teachings of the philosophers themselves usually had both an 'exoteric' and an 'esoteric' side, the latter leaving open the possibility of connection with a higher point of view, which in fact made itself clearly—though perhaps in some respects incompletely—apparent some centuries later among the Alexandrians. For 'profane' philosophy to be definitively constituted as such, it was necessary for exoterism alone to remain and for all esoterism simply to be denied, and it is precisely this that the movement inaugurated by the Greeks was to lead to in the modern world. The tendencies that found expression among the Greeks had to be pushed to the extreme, the undue importance given to rational thought had to grow even greater, before men could arrive at 'rationalism', a specifically modern attitude that consists in not merely ignoring, but expressly denying, everything of a supra-rational order. But let us not anticipate further, for we shall have to return to these consequences and to trace their development in a later part of this book.

In what has been said above, there is one thing that has particular bearing on the point of view with which we are concerned: it is that some of the origins of the modern world may be sought in 'classical' antiquity; the modern world is therefore not altogether wrong in

---

5. The relation is almost the same as that which exists in the Taoist doctrine between the 'gifted man' and the 'transcendent man' or 'true man'.

claiming to base itself on the Greco-Latin civilization and to be a continuation of it. At the same time, it must be remarked that the continuation is rather remote from, and unfaithful to, the original, for classical antiquity still possessed many things pertaining to the intellectual and spiritual order, to which no equivalent is to be found in the modern world; in any case, the two civilizations mark two quite different degrees in the progressive obscuration of true knowledge. One could indeed conceive of the decadence of the civilization of antiquity leading gradually, and without any breach of continuity, to a state more or less similar to that which we see today; but in fact this did not occur, and in the meanwhile there intervened another critical period for the West, a period that was at the same time one of those readjustments to which we have already referred.

This was the epoch that witnessed the rise and spread of Christianity, which coincided on the one hand with the dispersion of the Jews and on the other with the last phase of Greco-Latin civilization. We can pass over these events more rapidly, despite their importance, because they are more generally known than those we have previously spoken of, and also because their coincidence has received more attention, even by historians with the most superficial views. Attention has also frequently been drawn to certain features common to the decadence of the 'classical' world and to the present time; and, without wishing to push the parallel too far, it must be recognized that there are in reality striking resemblances. Purely 'profane' philosophy had gained ground: the appearance of skepticism on the one hand, and of Stoic and Epicurean moralism on the other, are sufficient to show to what point intellectuality had declined. At the same time, the ancient sacred doctrines, scarcely understood any longer by anyone, had degenerated through this lack of understanding into 'paganism' in the true sense of the word, that is to say they had become no more than 'superstitions', things which, having lost their profound meaning, survived for their own sake as merely outward manifestations. There were attempts to react against this decadence: Hellenism itself strove to acquire new vigor by the help of elements borrowed from those Eastern doctrines with which it was able to come in touch; but such means were no longer adequate; the Greco-Latin civilization had to end, and the readjustment had to come from outside and be realized in a totally different form. It was Christianity that accomplished this transformation; and it may be noted in this connection that the comparison that can be established in certain respects between that time and our own is, perhaps, one of the factors responsible for the disordered 'messianism' to be met with today. After the troubled period of the barbarian invasions, necessary to complete the destruction of the old order of things, a normal order was re-established for a period of some centuries; this period was that of the Middle Ages, of which the moderns—unable to understand its intellectuality—have so false an idea that it certainly appears to them far more alien and distant than classical antiquity.

For us, the real Middle Ages extend from the reign of Charlemagne to the opening of the fourteenth century, at which date a new decadence set in that has continued, through various phases and with gathering impetus, up to the present time. This date is the real starting-point of the modern crisis: it is the beginning of the disruption of Christendom, with which the Western civilization of the Middle Ages was essentially identified: at the same time, it marks the origin of the formation of 'nations' and the end of the feudal system, which was very closely linked with the existence of Christendom. The origin of the modern period must therefore be placed almost two centuries further back than is usual with historians; the Renaissance and Reformation were primarily results, made possible only by the preceding decadence; but, far from being a readjustment, they marked an even deeper falling off, consummating, as they did, the definitive rupture with the traditional spirit, the former in the domain of the arts and sciences, and the latter in that of religion itself, although this was the domain in which it might have seemed the most difficult to conceive of such a rupture.

As we have said on previous occasions, what is called the Renaissance was in reality not a re-birth but the death of many things; on the pretext of being a return to the Greco-Latin civilization, it merely took over the most outward part of it, since this was the only part that could be expressed clearly in written texts; and in any case, this incomplete restoration was bound to have a very artificial character, as it meant a re-establishment of forms whose real life had gone out of them centuries before. As for the traditional sciences of the Middle Ages, after a few final manifestations around this time, they disappeared as completely as those of distant civilizations long since destroyed by some cataclysm; and this time nothing was to arise in their place. Henceforth there was only 'profane' philosophy and 'profane' science, in other words, the negation of true intellectuality, the limitation of knowledge to its lowest order, namely, the empirical and analytical study of facts divorced from principles, a dispersion in an indefinite multitude of insignificant details, and the accumulation of unfounded and mutually destructive hypotheses and of fragmentary views leading to nothing other than those practical applications that constitute the sole real superiority of modern civilization—a scarcely enviable superiority, moreover, which, by stifling every other preoccupation, has given the present civilization the purely material character that makes of it a veritable monstrosity.

An altogether extraordinary fact is the rapidity with which Medieval civilization was completely forgotten; already in the seventeenth century, men had lost all idea of what it had been, and its surviving monuments no longer had any meaning for them, either intellectually or even esthetically; all this is proof enough of how far the general mentality had changed. We shall not here investigate the factors—and they are certainly complex—that contributed to bringing about a change so radical that it seems difficult to admit that it can have occurred spontaneously, without the intervention of some directing will whose exact nature must remain rather enigmatic. In this connection, one may note some very strange circumstances, such as the popularization at a certain moment, under the form of new discoveries, of things that had in reality been known for a very long time, but not generally disclosed, since the disadvantages of so doing ran the risk of outweighing the advantages.[6] It is also improbable that the legend alleging that the Middle Ages were a time of gloom, ignorance, and barbarism could have arisen and become accepted, or that the veritable falsification of history in which the

---

6. We will quote only two examples, which were to have consequences of the most serious kind: the pretended invention of printing, which had been known by the Chinese before the Christian era, and the 'official' discovery of America, with which continent far more extensive relations than is supposed had existed throughout the Middle Ages.

moderns have indulged, could have been accomplished in the absence of some preconceived idea; but we shall pursue this question no further, for, in whatever manner these processes may have taken place, our main concern for the moment is to make clear their results.

A word that rose to honor at the time of the Renaissance, and that summarized in advance the whole program of modern civilization is 'humanism'. Men were indeed concerned to reduce everything to purely human proportions, to eliminate every principle of a higher order, and, one might say, symbolically to turn away from the heavens under pretext of conquering the earth; the Greeks, whose example they claimed to follow, had never gone as far in this direction, even at the time of their greatest intellectual decadence, and with them utilitarian considerations had at least never claimed the first place, as they were very soon to do with the moderns. Humanism was the first form of what has subsequently become contemporary secularism; and, owing to its desire to reduce everything to the measure of man as an end in himself, modern civilization has sunk stage by stage until it has reached the level of the lowest elements in man and aims at little more than satisfying the needs inherent in the material side of his nature, an aim that is in any case quite illusory since it constantly creates more artificial needs than it can satisfy.

Will the modern world follow this fatal course right to the end, or will a new readjustment intervene once more, as it did in the case of the Greco-Latin decadence, before it reaches the bottom of the abyss into which it is being drawn? It would seem that a halt midway is no longer possible since, according to all the indications furnished by the traditional doctrines, we have in fact entered upon the last phase of the *Kali-Yuga*, the darkest period of this 'dark age', the state of dissolution from which it is impossible to emerge otherwise than by a cataclysm, since it is not a mere readjustment that is necessary at such a stage, but a complete renovation. Disorder and confusion prevail in every domain and have been carried to a point far surpassing all that has been known previously, so that, issuing from the West, they now threaten to invade the whole world; we know full well that their triumph can never be other than apparent and transitory, but such are the proportions which it has reached, that it would appear to be the sign of the gravest of all the crises through which mankind has passed in the course of its present cycle. Have we not arrived at that terrible age, announced in the Sacred Books of India, 'when the castes shall be mingled, when even the family shall no longer exist'? It is only necessary to look around in order to be convinced that this state is truly that of the world of today, and to see on all sides that profound degeneracy which the Gospel terms 'the abomination of desolation'. The gravity of the situation cannot be minimized; it should be envisaged such as it is, without optimism but also without pessimism, for as we have already said, the end of the old world will be also the beginning of a new one.

This gives rise to the question: what is the reason for a period such as the one in which we now live? Indeed, however abnormal present conditions may be when considered in themselves, they must nevertheless enter into the general order of things, that order which, according to a Far-Eastern formula, is made up of the sum of all disorders; the present age, however painful and troubled it may be, must also, like all the others, have its allotted place in the complete course of human development, and indeed the very fact of its being predicted by the traditional doctrines is indication enough that this is so. What we have already said regarding the general trend of a cycle of manifestation toward progressive materialization gives a direct explanation of such a state, and shows that what is abnormal and disordered from a particular point of view is nevertheless but the consequence of a law implied in a higher and more extensive point of view. We will add, without dwelling upon the question, that like every change of state the passage from one cycle to another can take place only in darkness; this is another law of great importance and with numerous applications; but for that very reason a detailed exposition of it would carry us too far from our subject.[7]

Nor is this all: the modern period must necessarily correspond with the development of certain possibilities that have lain within

---

7. This law was represented in the Eleusinian mysteries by the symbolism of the grain of wheat; the alchemists represented it by 'putrefaction' and the color black, which marks the beginning of the 'Great Work'; what the Christian mystics call the 'dark night of the soul' is the application of this law to the spiritual development of the being in its ascent to superior states; and it would be easy to indicate many other concordant applications.

the potentiality of the present cycle ever since its origin, and however low the rank of these possibilities in the hierarchy of the whole,
they like the others were bound to manifest themselves at their
appointed time. In this connection, it might be said that what,
according to tradition, characterizes the ultimate phase of a cycle is
the realization of all that has been neglected or rejected during the
preceding phases; and indeed, this is exactly the case with modern
civilization, which lives as it were only by that for which previous
civilizations had no use. To confirm this fact, it is enough to observe
how the genuine and traditional representatives of such of the more
ancient civilizations as have endured in the East up to the present
appraise Western sciences and their industrial applications. These
lower forms of knowledge, so worthless to anyone possessing
knowledge of a different and higher order, had nevertheless to be
realized, but this could not occur except at a stage where true intellectuality had disappeared. Such research, exclusively practical in
the narrowest sense of the word, was inevitable, but it could only be
carried out in an age at the opposite pole to primordial spirituality,
and by men so embedded in material things as to be incapable of
conceiving anything beyond them. The more they have sought to
exploit matter, the more they have become its slaves, thus dooming
themselves to ever increasing agitation without rule or objective, to
a dispersion in pure multiplicity leading to final dissolution.

Such, in broad outline and taking note only of essentials, is the
true explanation of the modern world; but let it be stated quite
clearly that this explanation can in no way be taken as a justification. An inevitable ill is nonetheless an ill, and even if good is to
come out of evil, this does not change the evil character of the evil
itself: we use the words 'good' and 'evil' here only to make ourselves
clear and without any specifically 'moral' intention. Partial disorders cannot but exist, since they are necessary elements in the total
order, but a period of disorder is in itself nevertheless comparable
to a monstrosity, which, though the consequence of certain natural
laws, is still a deviation and an error, or to a cataclysm, which,
though resulting from the normal course of events, is nevertheless a
subversion and an anomaly when viewed in itself. Modern civilization, like all things, has of necessity its reason for existing, and if

indeed it represents the state of affairs that terminates a cycle, one can say that it is what it should be and that it comes in its appointed time and place; but it should nonetheless be judged according to the words of the Gospel, so often misunderstood: 'Offense must needs come, but woe unto him through whom offense cometh.'

2

THE OPPOSITION
BETWEEN EAST
AND WEST

ONE OF THE MOST NOTICEABLE FEATURES of the modern world is the unmistakable gulf between East and West; although we have dealt with this question more fully elsewhere,[1] we must come back to it here in order to clarify certain of its aspects and to remove some misunderstandings. It is true that there have always been many and varied civilizations, each of which has developed in a manner natural to it and in conformity with the aptitudes of this or that people or race; but distinction does not mean opposition, and there can be equivalence of a sort between civilizations with very different forms, so long as they are all based on the same fundamental principles—of which they only represent applications varying in accordance with varied circumstances. This is the case with all civilizations that can be called normal or traditional, which comes to the same thing; there is no essential opposition between them, and such divergences as may exist are merely outward and superficial. On the other hand, a civilization that recognizes no higher principle, but is in reality based only on a negation of principles, is by this very fact ruled out from all mutual understanding with other civilizations, for if such understanding is to be profound and effective it can only come from above, that is to say from the very factor that

---

1. See *East and West*.

this abnormal and perverted civilization lacks. In the present state of the world then we have on the one hand all the civilizations that have remained faithful to the traditional standpoint—namely the civilizations of the East—and on the other a veritably anti-traditional civilization, namely that of the modern West.

There are, it is true, those who have denied that the division of mankind into East and West corresponds to any real difference; but it seems beyond doubt that, in the present time at any rate, this difference actually does exist. In the first place, the existence of a Western civilization, common to Europe and America, is a fact that everyone must recognize, whatever opinion may be held as to its value. The question is less simple with regard to the East, for there are actually several Eastern civilizations, and not one only; the distinction, and even the opposition, between the East and the West is however fully justified by the fact that these civilizations have certain common features, such as characterize what we have called a traditional civilization, and that these features are lacking in that of the West. That this is so is due to the fact that all the Eastern civilizations are alike traditional in character. To give a more definite idea of these civilizations, we will repeat here the general division between them that we have already laid down elsewhere, and which, though possibly somewhat simplified for someone wishing to enter into detail, is nevertheless correct in its main outlines: the Far East is represented essentially by the Chinese civilization, the Middle East (that is, India) by the Hindu, and the Near East by the Islamic. It should be added that in many respects this last is to be regarded as occupying an intermediate position between East and West, and that it has many features in common with Western civilization as it was in the Middle Ages; if one considers Islam in relation to the modern West, however, one cannot but see that it is just as opposed to it as are the properly Eastern civilizations, with which, from this point of view, it must therefore be classed.

The last remark raises an important point: there was no reason for opposition between East and West as long as there were traditional civilizations in the West as well as in the East; the opposition has meaning only as far as the modern West is concerned, for it is far more an opposition between two mentalities than between two more or less clearly defined geographical entities. In certain periods, of which the nearest to us is the medieval, the Western mentality was much more akin, in its more important features, to what is still the Eastern mentality than to what it has itself become in modern times; Western civilization was then comparable to the civilizations of the East in the same way as these are comparable to one another. During recent centuries there has occurred a great change that is far more serious than any of the deviations that may have occurred previously in periods of decadence, for it has proceeded to the point of an absolute reversal of the trend of human activity; and this change had its origin only in the West. When, therefore, in speaking of the world of today, we use the expression 'Western mentality', this means the same as the modern mentality; and since the other mentality has continued to exist only in the East, we can, also with reference to the present state of things, call it the Eastern mentality. These two terms, then, express nothing more than an actual fact; and, whereas one of the two mentalities has come into being during recent history and is in fact quite clearly Western, we do not wish to imply anything as to the source of the other, which was formerly common to East and West, for its origin must, if truth be told, merge with that of mankind itself, being the mentality that can be described as normal, if only for the reason that it has inspired more or less completely all the civilizations we know, with the exception of one only, that is to say, once again, the modern Western civilization.

Some people, who have doubtless not taken the trouble to read our books, have felt it incumbent on them to reproach us for having said that all traditional doctrines had their origin in the East, and that Western antiquity itself has, at all periods, always received its traditions from the East; we have never said any such thing, or even anything else that might suggest such an opinion, for the simple reason that we know quite well that it is untrue. Indeed, the traditional data themselves distinctly contradict such a statement: the explicit assertion is to be found everywhere that the primordial tradition of the present cycle comes from the hyperborean region; at a later time there were several secondary currents corresponding to different periods, and one of the most important of these, at least among those whose traces are still discernible, undoubtedly flowed from West to East. All this, however, refers to very far off times—such as are commonly called 'prehistoric'—with which we are not concerned here; what we do say is this: in the first place, the home of the primordial tradition has for a very long time now been in the East and it is there that the doctrinal forms that have issued most directly from it are to be found; secondly, in the present state of things, the true traditional spirit, with all that it implies, no longer has any authentic representatives except in the East.

This explanation would be incomplete without a reference, however brief, to certain proposals that have seen the light in various contemporary circles for restoring a 'Western tradition'. The only real interest afforded by these ideas is to show that there are people whose minds have ceased to be content with modern negation, and who, feeling the need for something that our own period cannot offer, see the possibility of an escape from the present crisis only in one way: through a return to tradition in one form or another. Unfortunately, such 'traditionalism' is not the same as the real traditional outlook, for it may be no more than a tendency, a more or less vague aspiration presupposing no real knowledge; and it is unfortunately true that, in the mental confusion of our times, this aspiration usually gives rise to fantastic and imaginary conceptions devoid of any serious foundation. Finding no authentic tradition on which to ground themselves, those affected by this aspiration go so far as to imagine pseudo-traditions that have never existed and that are as lacking in principles as that for which they are to be substituted; the whole modern confusion is reflected in these attempts, and whatever may be the intentions of their authors, their only result is to add still more to the general disequilibrium. From among conceptions of this kind, we will allude only to the so-called 'Western tradition' fabricated by certain occultists out of the most incongruous elements and intended primarily to compete with a no less imaginary 'Eastern tradition'—that of the Theosophists; we have spoken of these matters at sufficient length elsewhere, and prefer to pass on without further delay to the examination of other theories more worthy of attention, which reveal at least a desire to refer to traditions that have had a real existence.

We alluded above to the current of tradition that came from the West; accounts of Atlantis from ancient sources indicate its place of origin; after the disappearance of that continent in the last of the great cataclysms that have occurred in the past, there seems little doubt that the remnants of its tradition were carried into various regions, where they mingled with other already existing traditions, for the most part branches of the great Hyperborean tradition; and it is very possible that the doctrines of the Celts in particular were among the products of this fusion. We are far from disputing this; but let it not be forgotten that the real 'Atlantean' form disappeared thousands of years ago, together with the civilization to which it belonged and whose destruction can have come about only as the result of a perversion that may have been comparable in some respects to the one that confronts us today—with the important difference however that mankind had not yet entered upon the *Kali-Yuga*. Also, it should be remembered that the Atlantean tradition corresponded only to a secondary period in our cycle, and it would thus be a great mistake to seek to identify it with the primordial tradition out of which all the others have issued and which alone endures from the beginning to the end. It would be superfluous here to set forth all the data justifying these statements; we insist merely on the conclusion that it is impossible now to resuscitate an 'Atlantean' tradition, or to attach oneself more or less directly to it; there is a high degree of fantasy in attempts of this sort. It is nonetheless true that it may be of interest to investigate the origins of the elements that have come together to form later traditions, as long as, in so doing, all necessary precautions are taken to guard against illusion; but such investigations cannot lead to the resurrection of a tradition that is not adapted to any of the present conditions of our world.

There are others who wish to attach themselves to Celtism, and, since the model they take is less remote from our time, their purpose may seem less impracticable. But where can one find 'Celtism' today in a pure state and with sufficient vitality to be able to serve as a basis? We are not speaking of archeological or merely 'literary' reconstructions, several of which have appeared; we have in mind something very different. It is true that clearly recognizable and still usable elements of 'Celtism' have come down to us through various intermediaries, but these elements are very far from constituting a complete tradition; moreover, strange to say, even in the countries where it formerly existed, this tradition is now more completely forgotten than those of many other civilizations that never had a home there. Is there not here matter for reflection, at any rate for such as are not completely under the sway of a preconceived idea? We will go further: in all cases of this kind, when it is a question of vestiges left by vanished civilizations, it is impossible really to understand these vestiges except by comparison with similar elements in still extant traditional civilizations; and the same applies even to the Middle Ages, in which there are so many things that have lost their meaning for the modern West. It is only by establishing contact with still living traditions that what is capable of being revived can be made to live again; and this, as we have so often pointed out, is one of the greatest services that the East can render the West. We do not deny that a certain Celtic spirit has survived and can still manifest itself under various forms, as it has done at different times in the past; but when anyone tells us that there still exist spiritual centers where the Druid tradition is preserved in its entirety, we require them to show proof, and until they do so we consider it very doubtful, if not altogether incredible.

The truth is that the surviving Celtic elements were for the most part assimilated by Christianity in the Middle Ages; the legend of the 'Holy Grail', with all that it implies, is a particularly apt and significant example of this. Moreover, we think that if a Western tradition could be rebuilt it would be bound to take on a religious form in the strictest sense of this word, and that this form could only be Christian; for on the one hand the other possible forms have been too long foreign to the Western mentality, and on the other it is only in Christianity—and we can say still more definitely in Catholicism—that such remnants of a traditional spirit as still exist in the West are to be found. Every 'traditionalist' venture that ignores this fact is without foundation and therefore inevitably doomed to failure; it is self-evident that one can build only upon something that has a real existence, and that where there is lack of continuity, any reconstruction must be artificial and cannot endure. If it be objected that Christianity itself, in our time, is no longer understood in its profound meaning, we should reply that it has at least kept in its very form all that is needed to provide the foundation of which we have been speaking. The least fantastic venture, in fact the only one that does not come up against immediate impossibilities, would therefore be an attempt to restore something comparable to what existed in the Middle Ages, with the differences demanded by modifications in the circumstances; and for all that has been completely lost in the West, it would be necessary to draw upon the traditions that have been preserved in their entirety, as we stated above, and, having done so, to undertake the task of adaptation, which could be the work only of a powerfully established intellectual elite. All this we have said before, but it is useful to insist on it again because too many inconsistent fantasies are given free rein at present, and also because it is important to have it understood that, if the Eastern traditions in their own special forms can certainly be assimilated by an elite—which by its very definition must be beyond all forms—they certainly cannot be so by the mass of Western people, for whom they were not made, unless some unforeseen transformation takes place. If a Western elite comes to be formed, real knowledge of the Eastern doctrines will, for the reason that we have just given, be essential to it in the fulfillment of its functions; but the remainder, the majority of people, whose lot it will be to reap the benefits of its work, can quite well remain unaware of this, receiving the influence from it unwittingly and in any case by means that will be beyond their perception, though nonetheless real and effective. We have never said anything different, but we thought it well to repeat it here as clearly as possible, because, if we must not expect always to be understood by all, we at least endeavor to avoid having intentions ascribed to us that are in no way our own.

But it is the present state of things that concerns us most, so let us leave forecasts aside and dwell a moment longer on the suggestions that are at present to be met with for restoring a 'Western tradition'. There is one observation that would in itself suffice to show that these ideas are not in order: this is that they are almost always conceived from an attitude of more or less open hostility toward the East. It must be added that even those who wish to base themselves on Christianity are sometimes governed by this feeling: they seem set above all on finding points of opposition, which are really quite imaginary; and it is for this reason that we have encountered the absurd opinion that if the same things are found, expressed in almost identical form, in both Christianity and the Eastern doctrines, they nevertheless do not have the same meaning in the two cases, and have even contrary meanings! Those who make such assertions prove thereby that whatever may be their pretensions, they have not gotten very far in their understanding of the traditional doctrines, and have not perceived the fundamental identity underlying all the differences in outward form; and, even in cases where this identity is quite clear, they obstinately persist in not recognizing it. Also, the view they hold of Christianity itself is quite superficial, and could not correspond to the notion of a real traditional doctrine offering a complete synthesis that would embrace every domain; it is the basic principle that they lack, and in this they are affected far more than they may suppose by the modern outlook against which they wish to react; and when they have occasion to use the word 'tradition' they certainly do not give it the same meaning we do.

In the mental confusion that marks our times, the word 'tradition' itself has come to be applied indifferently to all sorts of things, often quite insignificant—for example, to mere customs with no wider bearing and sometimes of quite recent origin; we have remarked elsewhere on an abuse of the same kind in the use of the word 'religion'. These perversions of language must be distrusted, as they reflect a sort of degeneracy of the corresponding ideas; and the fact that somebody calls himself a 'traditionalist' does not prove that he knows, even vaguely, what tradition is in the true sense of the word. For our part, we refuse absolutely to give this name to anything that is of a purely human order; it is not superfluous to state this outright at a time when expressions such as 'traditional philosophy', to take an example, crop up at every turn. A philosophy, even though it be all that it should be, has no right to this designation, since it is entirely of the rational order even when it does not deny all that goes beyond this order. It is no more than a structure raised by human individuals without revelation or inspiration of any sort, which means, to cut a long story short, that it is essentially 'profane'. Moreover, despite all the illusions that some seem to cherish, the mentality of a race and an epoch is certainly not going to be put right by any merely 'bookish' science, but only by something very different from philosophical speculation, which, even at the best of times, is condemned by its very nature to remain outward and much more verbal than real. The lost tradition can be restored and brought to life again only by contact with the living traditional spirit, and, as we have already said, it is only in the East that this spirit is still fully alive. It is nonetheless true that the first necessity is the existence in the West of an aspiration toward a return to the traditional outlook, but this could hardly be more than a mere aspiration. The various movements of 'anti-modern' reaction that have already arisen—all very incomplete in our opinion—can only strengthen us in this conviction for, while doubtless excellent on their negative and critical side, they are nevertheless far from constituting a restoration of true intellectuality, and flourish only within the limits of a rather narrow mental horizon. They are at least something, however, in that they point to a frame of mind of which it would have been hard to find a trace even a few years ago; if all Westerners are no longer unanimous in contenting themselves with the exclusively material development of modern civilization, this may be a sign that for them not all hope of salvation has yet vanished.

Be this as it may, if the West should somehow return to its tradition, its opposition to the East would thereby be resolved and cease to exist, as it has its roots only in the Western deviation and is in reality nothing other than the opposition between the traditional and anti-traditional outlooks. Therefore, contrary to the views we have described above, one of the first results of a return to tradition would be to make an understanding with the East immediately feasible, such as is possible between all civilizations that possess comparable or equivalent elements—and only between such, since these elements form the only ground on which an effective understanding can be based. The real traditional outlook is always and everywhere essentially the same, whatever outward form it may take; the various forms that are specially suited to different mental conditions and different circumstances of time and place are merely expressions of one and the same truth; but this fundamental unity beneath apparent multiplicity can be grasped only by those who are able to take up a point of view that is truly intellectual. Moreover, it is in the intellectual realm that are to be found the principles from which everything else derives, either consequentially or by way of application; it is therefore on these principles that there must first of all be agreement if there is to be a really profound understanding, for they represent what is really essential; as soon as they are properly understood, agreement will come of itself. It should be added that knowledge of principles is essential knowledge, or metaphysical knowledge, in the true sense of the word, and is as universal as are the principles themselves; it is therefore entirely independent of all individual contingencies, which must on the contrary intervene as soon as one descends to applications; therefore this purely intellectual domain is the only one in which there is no need for the work of adaptation between different mentalities. Moreover, when the work has been done in this order, it remains only to develop its consequences, and agreement will also be reached in all other fields, since, as we have just said, it is on this that everything else, directly or indirectly, depends; on the other hand, agreement reached in any particular domain, outside the realm of principles, will always be unstable and precarious and much more like a diplomatic arrangement than a true understanding. This is why—we say again—a true understanding can come only from above and not from below; and this should be taken in a twofold sense: the work must begin from what is highest, that is, from principles, and descend gradually to the various orders of application, always keeping rigorously to the hierarchical dependence that exists between them; and it must also of necessity be the work of an elite in the truest and most complete meaning of this word: by this we mean exclusively an intellectual elite, and in reality, there can be no other.

These few considerations should explain how much is lacking in modern Western civilization, not only with regard to the possibility of an effective understanding with the Eastern civilizations, but also in itself, for it to be a normal and complete civilization; indeed, these two questions are so closely connected that they really form only one, and we have just given the reasons why this is the case. We have now to show more fully in what the anti-traditional outlook, which is really the modern outlook, consists, and what are the consequences that it bears within itself and that we see unfolding with a pitiless logic in present events—but before we pass on to this, one further remark is necessary. To be resolutely 'anti-modern' is not to be in any way 'anti-Western'; on the contrary, it only means making an effort to save the West from its own confusion. In any case, no Easterner who is faithful to his own tradition would view matters differently, and it is certain that there are far fewer opponents of the West as such—an attitude that makes no sense—than of the West insofar as it has become identified with modern civilization. There are those today who speak of a 'defense' of the West, which is odd, to say the least, considering that it is the West, as we shall see later on, that is threatening to submerge the whole of mankind in the whirlpool of its own confused activity; odd, we say, and completely unjustified if they mean, as they seem to (despite certain reservations), that this defense is to be against the East, for the true East has no thought of attacking or dominating anybody, and asks no more than to be left in independence and tranquillity—surely a not unreasonable demand. Actually, the truth is that the West really is in great need of defense, but only against itself and its own tendencies, which, if they are pushed to their conclusion, will lead inevitably to its ruin and destruction; it is therefore 'reform' of the West that is called for, and if this reform were what it should be—that is to say, a restoration of tradition—it would entail as a natural consequence an understanding with the East. For our own part, we ask no more than to contribute, as far as our means permit, both to the reform and to the understanding, if indeed there is still time, and if any such result can be attained before the arrival of the final catastrophe toward which modern civilization is heading. But even if it were already too late to avoid this catastrophe, the work done to this end would not be useless, for it would serve in any case to prepare, however distantly, the 'discrimination' of which we spoke at the beginning, and thereby to assure the preservation of those elements that must escape the shipwreck of the present world to become the germs of the future world.

3

KNOWLEDGE
AND ACTION

WE WILL NOW EXAMINE in greater detail one of the main aspects of the opposition that at present exists between the Eastern and the Western mentalities, and which, more generally speaking, coincides with the opposition between the traditional and the anti-traditional outlooks, as we have already explained. From one point of view—the one that is most important—this conflict reveals itself in the form of an opposition between contemplation and action, or, more strictly speaking, in a difference of opinion as to their relative importance. There are several different ways in which the relation between them can be regarded: are they really contraries, as seems to be the most general opinion, or are they not rather complementary to one another; or is not their relationship really one of hierarchical subordination rather than of co-ordination? Such are the various aspects of the question, and these aspects correspond to so many points of view, which, though far from being of equal importance, can all be justified in some respects, since each one of them corresponds to a certain order of reality.

We will begin with the shallowest and most outward point of view, that which consists in treating contemplation and action as being purely and simply opposed to one another, as contraries in the true sense of the word. It is beyond dispute that such an opposition does to all appearances exist; and yet, if this opposition were absolutely irreconcilable, there would be complete incompatibility between contemplation and action, and they could never be found together. But in fact this is not so; there is not, at least in normal cases, a people, nor possibly an individual, that can be exclusively contemplative or exclusively active. What is true is that there are two tendencies, the one or the other of which must almost inevitably predominate, so that the development of the one seems to take place at the expense of the other for the simple reason that human activity, in the widest sense of the term, cannot exert itself equally in all realms and all directions at the same time. It is this that gives the appearance of opposition; but a reconciliation must be possible between these contraries, or so-called contraries; as a matter of fact, one could say the same for all contraries, which cease to be such as soon as they are viewed from a higher level than the one where their opposition has its reality. Opposition or contrast means disharmony or disequilibrium, that is to say something which, as we have already made clear, can exist only from a relative, particular, and limited point of view.

To regard contemplation and action as complementary is therefore to adopt a point of view that is deeper and truer than the foregoing, since the opposition is reconciled and resolved, and the two terms to a certain extent balance one another. It would therefore seem to be a question of two equally necessary elements, which complete and support one another and constitute the twofold activity, inward and outward, of one and the same being, whether this be each man taken in himself or mankind viewed as a whole. This conception is certainly more harmonious and satisfying than the previous one; however, if one held to it exclusively, one would be tempted, in virtue of the correlation so established, to place contemplation and action on the same level, so that the only thing to do would be to strive to hold the balance between them as evenly as possible, without there ever being any question of the superiority of one over the other; but it is clear that this point of view is still inadequate, given that the question of superiority is and always has been raised, no matter in which way men may have tried to answer it.

The important point in this connection is not however mere predominance in practice, which is after all a matter of temperament or of race, but what might be called the right to predominance;

these two things are linked together only to a certain extent. Doubtless, recognition of superiority in one of the two tendencies will lead to its maximum development in preference to the other; but in practice it is nonetheless true that the particular capacity of each person has to be taken into account, and the places held by contemplation and action in the life of a man or a people will therefore always be to a great extent determined by his or their nature. It is obvious that the aptitude for contemplation is more widespread and more generally developed in the East, and probably nowhere more than in India, which can therefore be taken as representing most typically what we have called the Eastern mentality. On the other hand, it is beyond dispute that the aptitude for action, or rather the tendency resulting from this aptitude, is predominant among the peoples of the West, at least as far as the great majority of individuals is concerned. Even if this tendency were not exaggerated and perverted as it is at present, it would nevertheless continue to exist, so that in the West contemplation would always be bound to be the province of a much more restricted elite; it is for this reason that it is commonly said in India that, if the West returned to a normal state and had a regular social organization, there would be many Kshatriyas, but relatively few Brahmins.[1] If however the intellectual elite were effectually constituted and its supremacy recognized, this would be enough to restore everything to order, for spiritual power is in no way based on numbers, whose law is that of matter; besides—and this is a point of great importance—in ancient times, and especially in the Middle Ages, the natural bent of Westerners for action did not prevent them from recognizing the superiority of contemplation, or in other words, of pure intelligence. Why is it otherwise in modern times? Is it because Westerners have come to lose their intellectuality by over-developing their capacity for

1. Contemplation and action are in fact the respective functions of the two first castes, the Brahmins and the Kshatriyas; the relationship between them is the same as that between the spiritual authority and the temporal power; but we do not propose to go into this aspect of the question here, as it would require separate treatment. [See the author's *Spiritual Authority and Temporal Power.*]

action that they console themselves by inventing theories that set action above everything else, and even, as in the case of pragmatism, go so far as to deny that there exists anything of value beyond action; or is the contrary true, namely, that it is the acceptance of this point of view that has led to the intellectual atrophy we see today? In both instances—and if, as is probable, the truth lies between the two—the results are exactly the same; things have reached a point at which it is time to react; and this, be it said once more, is where the East can come to the help of the West (assuming the West is willing), not by thrusting upon it conceptions that are foreign to its mentality, as some persons seem to fear, but by helping it to recover the lost meaning of its own tradition.

The present antithesis between East and West may be said to consist in the fact that the East upholds the superiority of contemplation over action, whereas the modern West on the contrary maintains the superiority of action over contemplation. In this case, it is no longer a question of points of view, of which each may have its justification and be accepted as the expression of a relative truth, as was the case when we spoke of contemplation and action as being simply opposed or complementary to one another—with a consequent relationship of coordination between them. Relations of subordination are by their very nature irreversible, and the two conceptions are in fact contradictory and therefore exclusive of one another; if, therefore, one admits that there really is subordination, one conception must be true and the other false. But before proceeding to the root of the matter, let us note one more point: whereas the outlook that has survived in the East is found in all ages, as we observed above, the other attitude dates from only quite recently; and this, even apart from all other considerations, should in itself suggest that it is in some way abnormal. This impression is confirmed by the exaggeration into which the modern Western mentality falls through following its own inherent tendency, so that, not content with proclaiming on every occasion the superiority of action, men have come to the point of making action their sole preoccupation and of denying all value to contemplation, the true nature of which they ignore or entirely fail to understand. The Eastern doctrines, on the contrary, while asserting as clearly as possible the superiority, and even the transcendence, of contemplation over action, nonetheless allow action its legitimate place and make no difficulty in recognizing its importance in the order of human contingencies.[2]

The Eastern doctrines are unanimous, as also were the ancient doctrines of the West, in asserting that contemplation is superior to action, just as the unchanging is superior to change.[3] Action, being merely a transitory and momentary modification of the being, cannot possibly carry its principle and sufficient reason in itself; if it does not depend on a principle outside its own contingent domain, it is but illusion; and this principle, from which it draws all the reality it is capable of possessing—its existence and its very possibility—can be found only in contemplation, or, if one will, in knowledge, for these two terms are fundamentally synonymous, or at least coincide, since it is impossible in any way to separate knowledge from the process by which it is acquired.[4] Similarly change, in the widest sense of the word, is unintelligible and contradictory; in other words, it is impossible without a principle from which it proceeds and which, being its principle, cannot be subject to it, and is therefore necessarily unchanging; it was for this reason that, in the ancient world of the West, Aristotle asserted that there must be a 'unmoved mover' of all things. It is knowledge that serves as the 'unmoved mover' of action; it is clear that action belongs entirely to the world of change and 'becoming'; knowledge alone gives the possibility of leaving this world and the limitations that are inherent in it, and when it attains to the unchanging—as does principial or metaphysical knowledge, that is to say knowledge in its essence—it

2. Those who doubt the very real, though relative, importance assigned to action by the traditional doctrines of the East, and notably of India, have only to refer for evidence to the *Bhagavad Gītā*, which, as it is important to remember if one is to grasp its meaning aright, is a book destined especially for Kshatriyas.

3. It is in virtue of this relationship that the Brahmin is said to be the type of the stable being, whereas the Kshatriya is the type of the mobile or mutable being; thus, all beings in this world, depending on their nature, are in relation principally with one or the other, for there is a perfect correspondence between the cosmic and the human orders.

4. On the contrary, it should be noted that results in the realm of action, owing to its essentially momentary nature, are always separated from that which produces them, whereas knowledge bears its fruit in itself.

becomes itself possessed of immutability, for all true knowledge essentially consists in identification with its object. This is precisely what modern Westerners overlook: they admit nothing higher than rational or discursive knowledge, which is necessarily indirect and imperfect, being what might be described as reflected knowledge; and even this lower type of knowledge they are coming more and more to value only insofar as it can be made to serve immediate practical ends. Absorbed by action to the point of denying everything that lies beyond it, they do not see that this action itself degenerates, from the absence of any principle, into an agitation as vain as it is sterile. This indeed is the most conspicuous feature of the modern period: need for ceaseless agitation, for unending change, and for ever-increasing speed, matching the speed with which events themselves succeed one another. It is dispersion in multiplicity, and in a multiplicity that is no longer unified by consciousness of any higher principle; in daily life, as in scientific ideas, it is analysis driven to an extreme, endless subdivision, a veritable disintegration of human activity in all the orders in which this can still be exercised; hence the inaptitude for synthesis and the incapacity for any sort of concentration that is so striking in the eyes of Easterners. These are the natural and inevitable results of an ever more pronounced materialization, for matter is essentially multiplicity and division, and this—be it said in passing—is why all that proceeds from matter can beget only strife and all manner of conflicts between peoples as between individuals. The deeper one sinks into matter, the more the elements of division and opposition gain force and scope; and, contrariwise, the more one rises toward pure spirituality, the nearer one approaches that unity which can only be fully realized by consciousness of universal principles.

What is most remarkable is that movement and change are actually prized for their own sake, and not in view of any end to which they may lead; this is a direct result of the absorption of all human faculties in outward action whose necessarily fleeting character has just been demonstrated. Here again we have dispersion, viewed from a different angle and at a more advanced stage: it could be described as a tendency toward instantaneity, having for its limit a state of pure disequilibrium, which, were it possible, would coincide with the final dissolution of this world; and this too is one of the clearest signs that the final phase of the *Kali-Yuga* is at hand.

The same trend is noticeable in the scientific realm: research here is for its own sake far more than for the partial and fragmentary results it achieves; here we see an ever more rapid succession of unfounded theories and hypotheses, no sooner set up than crumbling to give way to others that will have an even shorter life—a veritable chaos amid which one would search in vain for anything definitive, unless it be a monstrous accumulation of facts and details incapable of proving or signifying anything. We refer here of course to speculative science, insofar as this still exists; in applied science there are on the contrary undeniable results, and this is easily understandable since these results bear directly on the domain of matter, the only domain in which modern man can boast any real superiority. It is therefore to be expected that discoveries, or rather mechanical and industrial inventions, will go on developing and multiplying more and more rapidly until the end of the present age; and who knows if, given the dangers of destruction they bear in themselves, they will not be one of the chief agents in the ultimate catastrophe, if things reach a point at which this cannot be averted?

Be that as it may, one has the general impression that, in the present state of things, there is no longer any stability; but while there are some who sense the danger and try to react to it, most of our contemporaries are quite at ease amid this confusion, in which they see a kind of exteriorized image of their own mentality. Indeed there is an exact correspondence between a world where everything seems to be in a state of mere 'becoming', leaving no place for the changeless and the permanent, and the state of mind of men who find all reality in this 'becoming', thus implicitly denying true knowledge as well as the object of that knowledge, namely transcendent and universal principles. One can go even further and say that it amounts to the negation of all real knowledge whatsoever, even of a relative order, since, as we have shown above, the relative is unintelligible and impossible without the absolute, the contingent without the necessary, change without the unchanging, and multiplicity without unity; 'relativism' is self-contradictory, for, in seeking to reduce everything to change, one logically arrives at a denial of the very existence of change; this was fundamentally the meaning of the famous arguments of Zeno of Elea. However, we have no wish to exaggerate and must add that theories such as these are not exclusively encountered in modern times; examples are to be found in Greek philosophy also, the 'universal flux' of Heraclitus being the best known; indeed, it was this that led the school of Elea to combat his conceptions, as well as those of the atomists, by a sort of *reductio ad absurdum*. Even in India, something comparable can be found, though, of course, considered from a different point of view from that of philosophy, for Buddhism also developed a similar character, one of its essential theses being the 'dissolubility of all things'.[5] These theories, however, were then no more than exceptions, and such revolts against the traditional outlook, which may well have occurred from time to time throughout the whole of the *Kali-Yuga*, were, when all is said and done, without wider influence; what is new is the general acceptance of such conceptions that we see in the West today.

It should be noted too that under the influence of the very recent idea of 'progress', 'philosophies of becoming' have, in modern times, taken on a special form that theories of the same type never had among the ancients: this form, although it may have multiple varieties, can be covered in general by the name 'evolutionism'. We need not repeat here what we have already said elsewhere on this subject; we will merely recall the point that any conception allowing for nothing other than 'becoming' is thereby necessarily a 'naturalistic' conception, and, as such, implies a formal denial of whatever

---

5. Soon after its origin, Buddhism in India became identified with one of the principal manifestations of the Kshatriyas' revolt against the authority of the Brahmins, and, as may be easily seen from what has gone before, there is in a general way a very direct connection between denial of any immutable principle and denial of the spiritual authority, between reduction of all reality to 'becoming' and assertion of the supremacy of the temporal power, whose proper domain is the world of action; and it could be shown that 'naturalist' or anti-metaphysical doctrines always arise when the element representing the temporal power takes the ascendancy in a civilization over that which represents the spiritual authority. [See *Spiritual Authority and Temporal Power*, in which Guénon treats this subject in considerable detail. Ed.]

lies beyond nature, in other words the realm of metaphysics—which is the realm of immutable and eternal principles. We may point out also, in speaking of these anti-metaphysical theories, that the Bergsonian idea of 'pure duration' corresponds exactly with that dispersion in instantaneity to which we alluded above; a pretended intuition modeled on the ceaseless flux of the things of the senses, far from being able to serve as an instrument for obtaining true knowledge, represents in reality the dissolution of all possible knowledge.

This leads us to repeat an essential point on which not the slightest ambiguity must be allowed to persist: intellectual intuition, by which alone metaphysical knowledge is to be obtained, has absolutely nothing in common with this other 'intuition' of which certain contemporary philosophers speak: the latter pertains to the sensible realm and in fact is sub-rational, whereas the former, which is pure intelligence, is on the contrary supra-rational. But the moderns, knowing nothing higher than reason in the order of intelligence, do not even conceive of the possibility of intellectual intuition, whereas the doctrines of the ancient world and of the Middle Ages, even when they were no more than philosophical in character, and therefore incapable of effectively calling this intuition into play, nevertheless explicitly recognized its existence and its supremacy over all the other faculties. This is why there was no rationalism before Descartes, for rationalism is a specifically modern phenomenon, one that is closely connected with individualism, being nothing other than the negation of any faculty of a supra-individual order. As long as Westerners persist in ignoring or denying intellectual intuition, they can have no tradition in the true sense of the word, nor can they reach any understanding with the authentic representatives of the Eastern civilizations, in which everything, so to speak, derives from this intuition, which is immutable and infallible in itself, and the only starting-point for any development in conformity with traditional norms.

4

SACRED AND
PROFANE SCIENCE

WE HAVE JUST SEEN that in civilizations of a traditional nature, intellectual intuition lies at the root of everything; in other words, it is the pure metaphysical doctrine that constitutes the essential, everything else being linked to it, either in the form of consequences or applications to the various orders of contingent reality. Not only is this true of social institutions, but also of the sciences, that is, branches of knowledge bearing on the domain of the relative, which in such civilizations are only regarded as dependencies, prolongations, or reflections of absolute or principial knowledge. Thus a true hierarchy is always and everywhere preserved: the relative is not treated as non-existent, which would be absurd; it is duly taken into consideration, but is put in its rightful place, which cannot but be a secondary and subordinate one; and even within this relative domain there are different degrees of reality, according to whether the subject lies nearer to or further from the sphere of principles.

Thus, as regards science, there are two radically different and mutually incompatible conceptions, which may be referred to respectively as traditional and modern. We have often had occasion to allude to the 'traditional sciences' that existed in antiquity and the Middle Ages and which still exist in the East, though the very idea of them is foreign to the Westerners of today. It should be added that every civilization has had 'traditional sciences' of its own and of a particular type. Here we are no longer in the sphere of universal principles, to which pure metaphysics alone belongs, but in the realm of adaptations. In this realm, by the very fact of its being a contingent one, account has to be taken of the whole complex of conditions, mental and otherwise, of a given people and, we may even say, of a given period in the existence of this people, since, as we have seen above, there are times at which 'readaptations' become necessary. These readaptations are no more than changes of form, which do not touch the essence of the tradition: with a metaphysical doctrine, only the expression can be modified, in a manner more or less comparable to a translation from one language into another; whatever be the forms it assumes for the sake of expressing itself— insofar as expression is possible—metaphysics remains one, just as truth itself is one. The case is different however when one passes to the realm of applications: with sciences, as with social institutions, we are in the world of form and multiplicity; therefore different forms can be said to constitute different sciences, even when the object of study remains at least partially the same. Logicians are apt to regard a science as being defined entirely by its object, but this is over-simplified and misleading; the angle from which the object is envisaged must also affect the definition of the science. The number of possible sciences is indefinite; it may well happen that several sciences study the same things, but under such different aspects and therefore by such different methods and with such different intentions that they are in reality different sciences. This is especially liable to be the case with the traditional sciences of different civilizations, which though mutually comparable nevertheless cannot always be assimilated to one another, and often cannot rightly be given the same name. The difference is even more marked if instead of comparing the different traditional sciences—which at least all have the same fundamental character—one tries to compare the sciences in general with the sciences of the modern world; it may sometimes seem at first sight that the object under study is the same in both cases, and yet the knowledge of it that the two kinds of science provide is so different that on closer examination one hesitates to say that they are the same in any respect.

A few examples may make our meaning clearer. To begin with, we will take a very general one, namely 'physics', as understood by the ancients and by the moderns respectively; here the profound difference between the two conceptions can be seen without leaving the Western world. The term 'physics', in its original and etymological sense, means precisely the 'science of nature' without qualification; it is therefore the science that deals with the most general laws of 'becoming', for 'nature' and 'becoming' are in reality synonymous, and it was thus that the Greeks, and notably Aristotle, understood this science. If there are more specialized sciences dealing with the same order of reality, they can amount to no more than 'specifications' of physics, dealing with one or another more narrowly defined sphere. Already, therefore, one can see the significant deviation of meaning to which the modern world has subjected the word 'physics', using it to designate exclusively one particular science among others, all of which are equally natural sciences, and this is an example of that process of subdivision we have already mentioned as being one of the characteristics of modern science. This 'specialization', arising from an analytical attitude of mind, has been pushed to such a point that those who have undergone its influence are incapable of conceiving of a science that deals with nature in its entirety. Some of the drawbacks of this specialization have not passed altogether unnoticed, especially the narrowness of outlook that is its inevitable outcome; but even those who perceive this most clearly seem nonetheless resigned to accept it as a necessary evil entailed by the accumulation of detailed knowledge such as no man could hope to take in at once; on the one hand, they have been unable to perceive that this detailed knowledge is insignificant in itself and not worth the sacrifice of synthetic knowledge which it entails, for synthetic knowledge, though it too is restricted to what is relative, is nevertheless of a much higher order; and on the other hand, they have failed to see that the impossibility of unifying the multiplicity of this detailed knowledge is due only to their refusal to attach it to a higher principle; in other words, it is due to a persistence in proceeding from below and from outside, whereas it is the opposite method that would be necessary if one wished to have a science of any real speculative value.

If one were to compare ancient physics, not with what the moderns call by this name, but with the totality of all the natural sciences as at present constituted—for this is its real equivalent—the first difference to be noticed would be the division it has undergone into multiple 'specialities' that are, so to speak, foreign to one another. This however is only the most outward side of the question, and it is not to be supposed that by joining together all these particular sciences one would arrive at an equivalent of ancient physics. The truth is that the point of view is quite different, and therein lies the essential difference between the two conceptions referred to above: the traditional conception, as we have said, attaches all the sciences to the principles of which they are the particular applications, and it is this attachment that the modern conception refuses to admit. For Aristotle, physics was only 'second' in its relation to metaphysics—in other words, it was dependent on metaphysics and was really only an application to the province of nature of principles that stand above nature and are reflected in its laws; and one can say the same for the Medieval cosmology. The modern conception on the contrary claims to make the various sciences independent, denying everything that transcends them, or at least declaring it to be 'unknowable' and refusing to take it into account, which in practice comes to the same thing. This negation existed *de facto* long before it was erected into a systematic theory under such names as 'positivism' or 'agnosticism', and it may truly be said to be the real starting-point of all modern science. It was however only in the nineteenth century that men began to glory in their ignorance—for to proclaim oneself an agnostic means nothing else—and claimed to deny to others any knowledge to which they had no access themselves; and this marked yet one more stage in the intellectual decline of the West.

By seeking to sever the connection of the sciences with any higher principle, under the pretext of assuring their independence, the modern conception robs them of all deeper meaning and even of all real interest from the point of view of knowledge; it can only lead them down a blind alley, by enclosing them, as it does, in a hopelessly limited realm.[1] Moreover, the development achieved in this

---

1. It should be noted that an analogous rupture has occurred in the social order, where the moderns claim to have separated the temporal from the spiritual. We do not mean to deny that the two are distinct, since they are in fact concerned with different provinces, just as are metaphysics and the sciences; but due to an error inherent in the analytical mentality, it has been forgotten that distinction does not mean separation. Because of this separation, the temporal power has lost its legitimacy—which is precisely what can be said, in the intellectual order, of the sciences.

realm is not a deepening of knowledge, as is commonly supposed, but on the contrary remains completely superficial, consisting only of the dispersion in detail already referred to and an analysis as barren as it is laborious; this development can be pursued indefinitely without coming one step closer to true knowledge. It must also be remarked that it is not for its own sake that, in general, Westerners pursue science; as they interpret it, their foremost aim is not knowledge, even of an inferior order, but practical applications, as can be deduced from the ease with which the majority of our contemporaries confuse science and industry, and from the number of those for whom the engineer represents the typical man of science; but this is connected with another question that we shall have to deal with more fully further on.

In assuming its modern form, science has lost not only in depth but also, one might say, in stability, for its attachment to principles enabled it to share in their immutability to the extent that its subject-matter allowed, whereas being now completely confined to the world of change, it can find nothing in it that is stable, and no fixed point on which to base itself; no longer starting from any absolute certainty, it is reduced to probabilities and approximations, or to purely hypothetical constructions that are the product of mere individual fantasy. Moreover, even if modern science should happen by chance to reach, by a roundabout route, certain conclusions that seem to be in agreement with some of the teachings of the ancient traditional sciences, it would be quite wrong to see in this a confirmation—of which these teachings stand in no need; it would be a waste of time to try to reconcile such utterly different points of view or to establish a concordance with hypothetical theories that may be completely discredited before many years are out.[2] As far as modern science is concerned, the conclusions in question can only belong to the realm of hypothesis, whereas the teachings of the traditional sciences had a very different character, coming as the

---

2. Within the religious realm, the same can be said about that type of 'apologetics' that claims to agree with the results of modern science—an utterly illusory undertaking and one that constantly requires revision; one that also runs the risk of linking religion with changing and ephemeral conceptions, from which it must remain completely independent.

indubitable consequences of truths known intuitively, and therefore infallibly, in the metaphysical order.[3] Modern experimentalism also involves the curious illusion that a theory can be proven by facts, whereas in reality the same facts can always be equally well explained by several different theories; some of the pioneers of the experimental method, such as Claude Bernard, have themselves recognized that they could interpret facts only with the help of preconceived ideas, without which they would remain 'brute facts' devoid of all meaning and scientific value.

Since we have been led to speak of experimentalism, the opportunity may be taken to answer a question that may be raised in this connection: why have the experimental sciences received a development in modern civilization such as they never had in any other? The reason is that these sciences are those of the sensible world, those of matter, and also those lending themselves most directly to practical applications; their development, proceeding hand in hand with what might well be called the 'superstition of facts', is therefore in complete accord with specifically modern tendencies, whereas earlier ages could not find sufficient interest in them to pursue them to the extent of neglecting, for their sake, knowledge of a higher order. It must be clearly understood that we are not saying that any kind of knowledge can be deemed illegitimate, even though it be inferior; what is illegitimate is only the abuse that arises when things of this kind absorb the whole of human activity, as we see them doing at present. One could even conceive, in a normal civilization, of sciences based on an experimental method being attached to principles in the same way as other sciences, and thus acquiring a real speculative value; if in fact this does not seem to have happened, it is because attention was turned for preference in a different direction, and also because, even when it was a question of studying the sensible world as far as it could appear interesting to do so, the traditional data made it possible to undertake this study more advantageously by other methods and from another point of view.

3. It would be easy to give examples of this: we will mention only one of the most striking: the difference in the conceptions of ether of Hindu cosmology and modern physics.

We said above that one of the characteristics of the present age is the exploitation of everything that had hitherto been neglected as being of insufficient importance for men to devote their time and energy to, but which nevertheless had to be developed before the end of the cycle, since the things concerned had their place among the possibilities destined to be manifested within it; such in particular is the case of the experimental sciences that have come into existence in recent centuries. There are even some modern sciences that represent, quite literally, residues of ancient sciences that are no longer understood: in a period of decadence, the lowest part of these sciences became isolated from all the rest, and this part, grossly materialized, served as the starting-point for a completely different development, in a direction conforming to modern tendencies; this resulted in the formation of sciences that have ceased to have anything in common with those that preceded them. Thus, for example, it is wrong to maintain, as is generally done, that astrology and alchemy have respectively become modern astronomy and modern chemistry, even though this may contain an element of truth from a historical point of view; it contains, in fact, the very element of truth to which we have just alluded, for, if the latter sciences do in a certain sense come from the former, it is not by 'evo-lution' or 'progress'—as is claimed—but on the contrary by degeneration. This seems to call for further explanation.

In the first place, it should be noted that the attribution of different meanings to the terms 'astrology' and 'astronomy' is relatively recent; the two words were used synonymously by the Greeks to denote the whole ground now covered by both. It would seem at first sight then that we have here another instance of one of those divisions caused by 'specialization' between what originally were simply parts of a single science. But there is a certain difference in this case, for whereas one of the parts, namely that representing the more material side of the science in question, has taken on an independent development, the other has on the contrary entirely disappeared. A measure of the truth of this lies in the fact that it is no longer known today what ancient astrology may have been, and that even those who have tried to reconstruct it have managed to create nothing more than parodies of it. Some have tried to assimilate it to a modern experimental science by using statistics and the calculation of probabilities, a method arising from a point of view which could not in any way be that of the ancient or medieval world. Others again confined their efforts to the restoration of an 'art of divination', which existed formerly, but which was merely a perversion of astrology in its decline and could at best be regarded as only a very inferior application unworthy of serious consideration, as may still be seen in the civilizations of the East.

The case of chemistry is perhaps even more clear and characteristic; and modern ignorance concerning alchemy is certainly no less than in the case of astrology. True alchemy was essentially a science of the cosmological order, and it was also applicable at the same time to the human order, by virtue of the analogy between the 'macrocosm' and the 'microcosm'; apart from this, it was constructed expressly so as to permit a transposition into the purely spiritual domain, and this gave a symbolical value and a higher significance to its teaching, making it one of the most typical and complete of the 'traditional sciences'. It is not from this alchemy, with which as a matter of fact it has nothing in common, that modern chemistry has sprung; the latter is only a corruption and, in the strictest sense of the word, a deviation from that science, arising, perhaps as early as the Middle Ages, from the incomprehension of persons who were incapable of penetrating the true meaning of the symbols and took everything literally. Believing that no more than material operations were in question, they launched out upon a more or less confused experimentation; it is these men, ironically referred to by the alchemists as 'puffers' and 'charcoal burners', who are the real forerunners of the present-day chemists; and thus it is that modern science is constructed from the ruins of ancient sciences with the materials that had been rejected and left to the ignorant and the 'profane'. It should be added that the so-called restorers of alchemy, of whom there are a certain number among our contemporaries, are merely continuing this same deviation, and that their research is as far from traditional alchemy as that of the astrologers to whom we have just referred is from ancient astrology; and that is why we have a right to say that the traditional sciences of the West are really lost for the moderns.

We will confine ourselves to these few examples, although it would be easy to give others taken from slightly different realms, and showing everywhere the same degeneration. One could show for instance that psychology as it is understood today—that is, the study of mental phenomena as such—is a natural product of Anglo-Saxon empiricism and of the eighteenth century mentality, and that the point of view to which it corresponds was so negligible for the ancient world that, even if it was sometimes taken incidentally into consideration, no one would have dreamed of making a special science of it, since anything of value that it might contain was transformed and assimilated in higher points of view. In quite a different field, one could show also that modern mathematics represents no more than the outer crust or 'exoteric' side of Pythagorean mathematics; the ancient idea of numbers has indeed become quite unintelligible to the moderns, because, here too, the higher portion of the science, which gave it its traditional character and therewith a truly intellectual value, has completely disappeared—a case that is very similar to that of astrology. But to pass all the sciences in review, one after another, would be somewhat tedious; we consider that we have said enough to make clear the nature of the change to which modern sciences owe their origin, a change that is the direct opposite of 'progress', amounting indeed to a veritable regression of intelligence. We will now return to considerations of a general order concerning the purposes served respectively by the traditional sciences and the modern sciences, so as to show the profound difference that exists between the real purpose of the one and of the other.

According to the traditional conception, any science is of interest less in itself than as a prolongation or secondary branch of the doctrine, whose essential part consists in pure metaphysics.[4] Actually, though every science is legitimate as long as it keeps to the place that belongs to it by virtue of its own nature, it is nevertheless easy to understand that knowledge of a lower order, for anyone who possesses knowledge of a higher order, is bound to lose much of its interest. It remains of interest only, so to speak, as a function of

---

4. This is expressed, for example, in such a designation as *upaveda*, used in India for certain traditional sciences and showing their subordination to the *Veda*, that is, sacred knowledge.

principial knowledge, that is, insofar as it is capable, on the one hand, of reflecting this knowledge in a contingent domain, and on the other, of leading to this knowledge itself, which, in the case that we have in mind, must never be lost sight of or sacrificed to more or less accidental considerations. These are the two complementary functions proper to the traditional sciences: on the one hand, as applications of the doctrine, they make it possible to link the different orders of reality and to integrate them into the unity of a single synthesis, and on the other, they constitute, at least for some, and in accordance with their individual aptitudes, a preparation for a higher knowledge and a way of approach to it—forming by virtue of their hierarchical positioning, according to the levels of existence to which they refer, so many rungs as it were by which it is possible to climb to the level of pure intellectuality.[5] It is only too clear that modern sciences cannot in any way serve either of these purposes; this is why they can be no more than 'profane science', whereas the 'traditional sciences', through their connection with metaphysical principles, are effectively incorporated in 'sacred science'.

The co-existence of the two roles we have just mentioned does not imply a contradiction or a vicious circle, as those who take a superficial view of the question might suppose, but it is a point calling for further discussion. It could be explained by saying that there are two points of view, one descending and the other ascending, one corresponding to the unfolding of knowledge starting from principles and proceeding to applications further and further removed from them, and the other implying a gradual acquisition of this knowledge, proceeding from the lower to the higher, or, if preferred, from the outward to the inward. The question does not have to be asked, therefore, whether the sciences should proceed from below upward or from above downward, or whether, to make their existence possible, they should be based on knowledge of principles or

---

5. In our study *The Esoterism of Dante* we spoke of the symbolism of the ladder, the rungs of which correspond, in several traditions, to certain sciences and, at the same time, to states of being; this necessarily implies that these sciences were not regarded in a merely 'profane' manner, as in the modern world, but allowed of a transposition bestowing on them a real initiatic significance.

on knowledge of the sensible world; this question can arise from the point of view of 'profane' philosophy and seems, indeed, to have arisen more or less explicitly in this domain in ancient Greece, but it cannot exist for 'sacred science', which can be based only on universal principles; the reason why this is pointless in the latter case is that the prime factor here is intellectual intuition, which is the most direct of all forms of knowledge, as well as the highest, and which is absolutely independent of the exercise of any faculty of the sensible or even the rational order. Sciences can only be validly constituted as 'sacred sciences' by those who, before all else, are in full possession of principial knowledge and are thereby qualified to carry out, in conformity with the strictest traditional orthodoxy, all the adaptations required by circumstances of time and place. However, when these sciences have been so established, their teaching may follow an inverse order: they then serve as it were as 'illustrations' of pure doctrine, which they render more easily accessible to certain minds, and the fact that they are concerned with the world of multiplicity gives them an almost indefinite variety of points of view, adapted to the no less great variety of the individual aptitudes of those whose minds are still limited to that same world of multiplicity. The ways leading to knowledge may be extremely different at the lowest degree, but they draw closer and closer together as higher levels are reached. This is not to say that any of these preparatory degrees are absolutely necessary, since they are mere contingent methods having nothing in common with the end to be attained; it is even possible for some persons, in whom the tendency to contemplation is predominant, to attain directly to true intellectual intuition without the aid of such means;[6] but this is a more or less exceptional case, and in general it is accepted as being necessary to proceed upward gradually. The whole question may also be illustrated by means of the traditional image of the 'cosmic wheel': the circumference in reality exists only in virtue of the center, but the beings that stand

6. This is why, according to Hindu doctrine, Brahmins should keep their minds constantly turned toward supreme knowledge, whereas Kshatriyas should rather apply themselves to a study of the successive stages by which this is gradually to be reached.

upon the circumference must necessarily start from there or, more precisely, from the point thereon at which they actually find themselves, and follow the radius that leads to the center. Moreover, because of the correspondence that exists between all the orders of reality, the truths of a lower order can be taken as symbols of those of higher orders, and can therefore serve as 'supports' by which one may arrive at an understanding of these; and this fact makes it possible for any science to become a sacred science, giving it a higher or 'anagogical' meaning deeper than that which it possesses in itself.[7]

Every science, we say, can assume this character, whatever may be its subject-matter, on the sole condition of being constructed and regarded from the traditional standpoint; it is only necessary to keep in mind the degrees of importance of the various sciences according to the hierarchical rank of the diverse realities studied by them; but whatever degree they may occupy, their character and functions are essentially similar in the traditional conception. What is true of the sciences is equally true of the arts, since every art can have a truly symbolic value that enables it to serve as a support for meditation, and because its rules, like the laws studied by the sciences, are reflections and applications of fundamental principles: there are then in every normal civilization 'traditional arts', but these are no less unknown to the modern West than are the 'traditional sciences'.[8] The truth is that there is really no 'profane realm' that could in any way be opposed to a 'sacred realm'; there is only a 'profane point of view', which is really none other than the point of view of ignorance.[9] This is why 'profane science', the science of the

7. This is the purpose, for example, of the astronomical symbolism so commonly used in the various traditional doctrines; and what we say here can help to indicate the true nature of ancient astrology.

8. The art of the medieval builders can be cited as a particularly remarkable example of these traditional arts, whose practice moreover implied a real knowledge of the corresponding sciences.

9. To see the truth of this, it is sufficient to note facts such as the following: cosmogony, one of the most sacred of the sciences—and one that has its place in all the inspired books, including the Hebrew Bible—has become for the modern world a subject for completely 'profane' hypotheses; the domain of the science is indeed the same in both cases, but the point of view is utterly different.

moderns, can as we have remarked elsewhere be justly styled 'ignorant knowledge', knowledge of an inferior order confining itself
entirely to the lowest level of reality, knowledge ignorant of all that
lies beyond it, of any aim more lofty than itself, and of any principle
that could give it a legitimate place, however humble, among the
various orders of knowledge as a whole. Irremediably enclosed in
the relative and narrow realm in which it has striven to proclaim
itself independent, thereby voluntarily breaking all connection with
transcendent truth and supreme wisdom, it is only a vain and illusory knowledge, which indeed comes from nothing and leads to
nothing.

This survey will suffice to show how great is the deficiency of the
modern world in the realm of science, and how that very science of
which it is so proud represents no more than a deviation and, as it
were, a downfall from true science, which for us is absolutely identical with what we have called 'sacred' or 'traditional' science. Modern science, arising from an arbitrary limitation of knowledge to a
particular order—the lowest of all orders, that of material or sensible reality—has lost, through this limitation and the consequences
it immediately entails, all intellectual value; as long, that is, as one
gives to the word 'intellectuality' the fullness of its real meaning,
and refuses to share the 'rationalist' error of assimilating pure intelligence to reason, or, what amount to the same thing, of completely
denying intellectual intuition. The root of this error, as of a great
many other modern errors—and the cause of the entire deviation of
science that we have just described—is what may be called 'individualism', an attitude indistinguishable from the anti-traditional attitude itself and whose many manifestations in all domains constitute
one of the most important factors in the confusion of our time; we
shall therefore now study this individualism more closely.

5

INDIVIDUALISM

BY INDIVIDUALISM we mean the negation of any principle higher than individuality, and the consequent reduction of civilization, in all its branches, to purely human elements; fundamentally, therefore, individualism amounts to the same thing as what, at the time of the Renaissance, was called 'humanism'; it is also the characteristic feature of the 'profane point of view' as we have described it above. Indeed these are but different names for the same thing; and we have also shown that this 'profane' outlook coincides with the anti-traditional outlook that lies at the root of all specifically modern tendencies. That is not to say, of course, that this outlook is entirely new; it had already appeared in a more or less pronounced form in other periods, but its manifestations were always limited in scope and apart from the main trend, and they never went so far as to overrun the whole of a civilization, as has happened during recent centuries in the West. What has never been seen before is the erection of an entire civilization on something purely negative, on what indeed could be called the absence of principle; and it is this that gives the modern world its abnormal character and makes of it a sort of monstrosity, only to be understood if one thinks of it as corresponding to the end of a cyclical period, as we have already said. Individualism, thus defined, is therefore the determining cause of the present decline of the West, precisely because it is, so to speak, the mainspring for the development of the lowest possibilities of mankind, namely those possibilities that do not require the intervention of any supra-human element and which, on the contrary, can only expand freely if every supra-human element be absent, since they stand at the antipodes of all genuine spirituality and intellectuality.

Individualism implies, in the first place, the negation of intellectual intuition—inasmuch as this is essentially a supra-individual faculty—and of the knowledge that constitutes the true province of this intuition, namely metaphysics understood in its true sense. That is why everything that modern philosophers understand by the word metaphysics—if they admit the existence of anything at all under this name—is completely foreign to real metaphysics; it consists indeed of nothing but rational constructs or imaginative hypotheses, and thus purely individual conceptions, most of which bear only on the domain of 'physics', or in other words of nature. Even if any question is touched upon that could really belong to the metaphysical order, the manner in which it is envisaged and treated reduces it to the level of 'pseudo-metaphysics', and precludes any real or valid solution. It would seem, indeed, as if the philosophers are much more interested in creating problems, however artificial and illusory they may be, than in solving them; and this is but one aspect of the irrational love of research for its own sake, that is to say, of the most futile agitation in both the mental and the corporeal domains. It is also an important consideration for these philosophers to be able to put their name to a 'system', that is, to a strictly limited and circumscribed set of theories, which shall belong to them and be exclusively their creation; hence the desire to be original at all costs, even if truth should have to be sacrificed to this 'originality': a philosopher's renown is increased more by inventing a new error than by repeating a truth that has already been expressed by others. This form of individualism, the begetter of so many 'systems' that contradict one another even when they are not contradictory in themselves, is to be found also among modern scholars and artists; but it is perhaps in philosophy that the intellectual anarchy to which it inevitably gives rise is most apparent.

In a traditional civilization it is almost inconceivable that a man should claim an idea as his own; and in any case, were he to do so, he would thereby deprive it of all credit and authority, reducing it to the level of a meaningless fantasy: if an idea is true, it belongs equally to all who are capable of understanding it; if it is false, there is no credit in having invented it. A true idea cannot be 'new', for truth is not a product of the human mind; it exists independently of us, and all we have to do is to take cognizance of it; outside this knowledge there can be nothing but error: but do the moderns on the whole care much about truth, or do they even know what it is? Here again words have lost their real meaning, inasmuch as some people—for instance contemporary pragmatists—go so far as to misappropriate the word 'truth' for what is simply practical utility, that is to say for something that is quite foreign to the intellectual order. The logical outcome of the modern deviation is precisely the negation of truth, as well as of the intelligence of which truth is the object. But let us not anticipate further, and on this point merely say that the kind of individualism of which we have been speaking is the chief source of the illusions about the importance of so-called 'great men'; to be a 'genius', in the profane sense of the word, amounts to very little, and is utterly incapable of making up for the lack of true knowledge.

As we are speaking of philosophy, we shall mention some of the consequences of individualism in this field, though without entering into every detail: first of all there was the negation of intellectual intuition and the consequent raising of reason above all else, this purely human and relative faculty being treated as the highest part of the intelligence, or even as coinciding with the whole of the intelligence; this is what constitutes rationalism, whose real founder was Descartes. This limitation of intelligence was however only a first stage; before long, reason itself was increasingly relegated to mainly practical functions, in proportion as applications began to predominate over such sciences as might still have kept a certain speculative character; and Descartes himself was already at heart much more concerned with these practical applications than with pure science. More than this: individualism inevitably implies naturalism, since all that lies beyond nature is, for that very reason, out of reach of the individual as such; naturalism and the negation of metaphysics are indeed but one and the same thing, and once intellectual intuition is no longer recognized, no metaphysics is any longer possible; but whereas some persist in inventing a 'pseudo-metaphysics' of one kind or another, others—with greater frankness—assert its impossibility; from this has arisen 'relativism' in all its forms, whether it be the 'criticism' of Kant or the 'positivism' of Auguste Comte; and since reason itself is quite relative, and can deal validly only with a domain that is equally relative, it is true to say that 'relativism' is the only logical outcome of rationalism. By this means, however, rationalism was to bring about its own destruction: 'nature' and 'becoming', as we said above, are in reality synonymous; a consistent naturalism can therefore only be one of the 'philosophies of becoming', already mentioned, of which the specifically modern type is evolutionism; it was precisely this that finally turned against rationalism, by accusing reason of being unable to deal adequately, on the one hand, with what is solely change and multiplicity, and, on the other, with the indefinite complexity of sensible phenomena. This is in fact the position taken up by one form of evolutionism, namely Bergsonian intuitionism, which in fact is not less individualistic and anti-metaphysical than rationalism itself; indeed, although it is just in its criticism of the latter, it sinks even lower, by appealing to a faculty that is really infra-rational, to a vaguely defined sensory intuition more or less mixed up with imagination, instinct, and sentiment. It is highly significant that there is no longer any question here of 'truth', but only of a 'reality' that is reduced exclusively to the sensible order and conceived as something essentially changing and unstable; with such theories, intelligence is reduced to its lowest part, and reason itself is no longer admitted except insofar as it is applied to fashioning matter for industrial uses. After this there remained but one step: the total denial of intelligence and knowledge altogether and the substitution of 'utility' for 'truth'. This step was pragmatism, to which we have just referred; here we are no longer even in the merely human domain as with rationalism, for the appeal to the 'subconscious', which marks the complete reversal of the normal hierarchy, brings us down in fact to the infra-human. This, in its main outlines, is the course that 'profane' philosophy, left to itself and claiming to limit all knowledge to its own horizon, was bound to tread, and has indeed trodden: as long as there existed a higher knowledge, nothing of this sort could happen, for philosophy was bound at least to respect that of which it was ignorant, but whose existence it could not deny; but when this higher knowledge had disappeared, its negation, already a fact, was soon erected into a theory, and it is from this that all modern philosophy has sprung.

But we have dwelt long enough on philosophy, to which it would be wrong to attribute overmuch importance, whatever place it may appear to hold in the modern world; from our point of view, it is interesting mainly because it expresses, in as clear a form as possible, the tendencies of this or that period, much more than it actually creates them; and even if it can be said to direct them to a certain extent, it does so only secondarily and when they are already formed. Thus, for instance, it is certain that all modern philosophy has its origin in Descartes; but the influence exerted by him, firstly on his own time, and then on those that followed—an influence not confined to philosophers alone—would not have been possible had his conceptions not been in agreement with already existing tendencies which, as a matter of fact, prevailed among his contemporaries in general; the modern mentality is reflected in Cartesianism and, through Cartesianism, it acquired a clearer knowledge of itself than it possessed before. Moreover, if a movement in any domain is as conspicuous as Cartesianism has been in that of philosophy, it is always rather more as a result than as a cause; it is not something spontaneous, but the result of a wider underlying activity. If a man like Descartes is especially representative of the modern deviation, so that to some extent and from a certain point of view one can say that he personifies it, it remains nonetheless true that he is not its sole or first originator and that one would have to go much further back to trace its source. In the same way the Renaissance and the Reformation, which are usually considered to be the first great manifestations of the modern mentality, completed the breach with tradition rather than provoked it; for us, the beginning of this breach is to be found in the fourteenth century, and it is at this date, and not a century or two later, that the beginning of modern times should be fixed.

This breach with tradition calls for further comment, for it is precisely this that produced the modern world, whose characteristics could all be summed up under one single heading, namely opposition to the traditional spirit; and negation of tradition, once again, is the same as individualism. This, indeed, is in perfect accord with what has already been said, since it is intellectual intuition and pure metaphysical doctrine that constitute the very principle of every traditional civilization; once the principle is denied, all its consequences must be denied also, at least implicitly, and thereby everything that really merits the name of tradition is destroyed at one blow. We have already seen how this process has worked in the case of the sciences, and we shall therefore not return to them but pass on to another province, in which the manifestations of the anti-traditional outlook strike the eye perhaps even more immediately, since the changes produced have had a direct effect on the great mass of the people in the West. Actually, the traditional sciences of the Middle Ages were confined to a not very numerous elite, and some of them were even a monopoly of strictly closed schools, and therefore constituted an esoterism in the true sense of the word; but there was also a part of the tradition that belonged to all without distinction, and it is of this outward part that we now wish to speak. At that time, the tradition of the West bore outwardly a specifically religious form, being in fact represented by Catholicism; it is therefore in the realm of religion that we shall have to consider the revolt against the traditional outlook, a revolt which, when it had acquired a definite form, became known as Protestantism; it is not difficult to see that this is a manifestation of individualism; indeed one could call it individualism as applied to religion. Protestantism, like the modern world, is built upon mere negation, the same negation of principles that is the essence of individualism; and one can see in it one more example, and a most striking one, of the state of anarchy and dissolution that has arisen from this negation.

Individualism necessarily implies the refusal to accept any authority higher than the individual, as well as any means of knowledge higher than individual reason; these two attitudes are inseparable. Consequently the modern outlook was bound to reject all spiritual authority in the true sense of the word, namely authority that is based on the supra-human order, as well as any traditional organization, that is, any organization based essentially on this authority, whatever be its form—for the form will naturally vary with each civilization. This is what in fact did happen: Protestantism denied the authority of the organization qualified to interpret legitimately the religious tradition of the West and in its place claimed to set up 'free criticism', that is to say any interpretations resulting from private judgement, even that of the ignorant and incompetent, and based exclusively on the exercise of human reason. What happened in the realm of religion was therefore analogous to the part to be played by rationalism in philosophy: the door was left open to all manner of discussions, divergencies, and deviations; and the result could not but be dispersion in an ever growing multitude of sects, each of which represents no more than the private opinion of certain individuals. As it was impossible under such conditions to come to an agreement on doctrine, this was soon thrust into the background, and the secondary aspect of religion, namely morality, came to the fore: hence the degeneration into moralism so patent in present-day Protestantism. There thus arose a phenomenon, parallel to that to which we have referred in the case of philosophy, as an inevitable consequence of the dissolution of doctrine and the disappearance from religion of its intellectual elements. From rationalism, religion was bound to sink into sentimentalism, and it is in the Anglo-Saxon countries that the most striking examples of this are to be found. What remains is therefore no longer even a dwindling and deformed religion, but simply 'religiosity', that is to say vague and sentimental aspirations unjustified by any real knowledge: to this final stage correspond theories such as that of the 'religious experience' of William James, which goes to the point of finding in the 'subconscious' man's means of entering into communication with the divine. At this stage the final products of religious and of philosophical decline mingle together and 'religious experience' becomes merged in pragmatism, in the name of which a limited God is stipulated as being more 'advantageous' than an infinite God, insofar as one can feel for him sentiments comparable to those one would feel for a higher man. At the same time, the appeal to the 'subconscious' joins hands with modern spiritualism and all those 'pseudo-religions' characteristic of our age. In another direction, Protestant moralism, having gradually eliminated all doctrinal basis, has ended by degenerating into what is called 'lay morality', which counts among its adherents the representatives of all the varieties of 'liberal Protestantism', as well as the open enemies of every religious idea; fundamentally, both groups are guided by the same tendencies, and the only difference is that not all go equally far in the logical development of everything that these tendencies imply.

Actually, religion being essentially a form of tradition, the anti-traditional outlook cannot help being anti-religious; it begins by denaturing religion and, when it can, ends by suppressing it entirely. Protestantism is illogical: while doing all it can to 'humanize' religion, it nevertheless, in theory at least, retains revelation, which is a supra-human element. It does not dare carry its negation to the logical conclusion but, by subjecting revelation to all the discussions resulting from purely human interpretations, it does in fact reduce it to next to nothing; and seeing, as one does, people who persist in calling themselves Christian even though they deny the very divinity of Christ, one cannot avoid the supposition that they are much nearer to complete negation than to real Christianity, although they may not realize the fact. Such contradictions, however, should not occasion too much surprise, for they are in every field one of the symptoms of the disorder and confusion of our times, just as the incessant subdivision of Protestantism is one of the many manifestations of that dispersion in multiplicity which, as we have shown, is to be found everywhere in modern life and science. Moreover, it is natural that Protestantism, owing to the spirit of negation by which it is animated, should have given birth to that destructive 'criticism' which, in the hands of the so-called 'historians of religion', has been turned into a weapon against all religion, so that, while claiming to recognize no other authority than that of the Sacred Books, the Protestant movement has in this way contributed very largely toward the destruction of this very authority—that is to say of the minimum of tradition that it still retained. Once started, the revolt against the traditional outlook could not be stopped halfway.

An objection might here be raised: although it broke away from the Catholic organization, might not Protestantism, in that it continued to admit the validity of the Sacred Books, have preserved the traditional doctrine contained therein? But the introduction of 'free criticism' completely refutes such a hypothesis, since it opens the door to all manner of individual fantasies; moreover, the preservation of the doctrine presupposes an organized traditional teaching to keep alive the orthodox interpretation, and in actual fact this teaching has, in the Western world, been identified with Catholicism. No doubt other civilizations may possess organizations of very different form to fulfill the corresponding function, but it is the civilization of the West, with all the conditions peculiar to it, that concerns us here. It would be to no purpose therefore to plead that there is no institution comparable to the Papacy in India; the case is quite different there, in the first place because its tradition does not take the form of a religion in the Western sense of the word, so that the means by which it is preserved and transmitted cannot be the same, and secondly because—the Hindu mentality being quite different from the European—the Hindu tradition possesses within itself an inherent power such as the European tradition could not enjoy without the support of an organization much more rigidly defined in its outward constitution. We have already said that the Western tradition has necessarily borne a religious form since the introduction of Christianity. It would take too long to explain here all the reasons for this, reasons that could moreover not be fully understood without entering into rather complex considerations, but it is an actual fact with which one cannot refuse to reckon;[1] and once admitted, one must also admit all the consequences it entails with regard to an organization suited to this kind of traditional form.

It is moreover quite certain, as we showed above, that it is in Catholicism alone that all that may still remain of the traditional spirit in the West has been preserved; but does this mean that in Catholicism at least one can speak of an integral conservation of tradition completely untainted by the modern spirit? Unfortunately this does not appear to be the case; or, more precisely, if the deposit of tradition has remained intact, which is in itself much, it is doubtful whether its deeper meaning is fully understood, even by a restricted elite, which, if it existed, would doubtless show itself

---

1. Moreover, according to the Gospel, this state is to continue until 'the Last Day', that is to say until the end of the present cycle.

either in action or in influence, neither of which, in fact, is any-where to be seen. Most probably therefore there is only what might be termed a preservation of the tradition in a latent state, in which state it is always possible for those who are capable of it to redis-cover its meaning, even though no one may be fully aware of it at the present time; moreover, outside the religious domain, scattered here and there in the Western world, there are also many signs or symbols descended from ancient traditional doctrines and pre-served without being understood. In such cases, contact with the fully living traditional spirit is necessary to awaken what has thus fallen into a kind of sleep, and to restore the lost understanding; and, be it said once more, it is mainly in this respect that the West will require help from the East if it is to recover knowledge of its own tradition.

What we have just said refers to the possibilities which Catholi-cism, through its principle, faithfully and unalterably contains; with Catholicism, therefore, the influence of the modern outlook is unable to do more than prevent certain things from being effectively understood, at least for a certain time. However, one would have to admit a more positive effect of the modern outlook on the present state of Catholicism if one judged it by the way in which the great majority of its adherents understand it today; that is, if one can use the expression 'positive' for something that is, in reality, essentially negative. In saying this, we are thinking not only of more or less specific movements, such as that which was actually called 'modern-ism' and which was nothing other than an attempt—happily frustrated—to smuggle the anti-traditional outlook into the Catho-lic church itself; we are thinking more particularly of a state of mind that is more general and diffused, less easily definable, and therefore still more dangerous, and whose great danger lies in the fact that those who are affected by it are often unaware of its existence. It is possible to think oneself sincerely religious and not be at all reli-gious at heart; it is even possible to consider oneself a 'traditionalist' without having the least notion of the real traditional spirit; and this is one more symptom of the mental confusion of our time. The state of mind we are referring to is primarily one that consists, so to speak, in 'minimizing' religion, in treating it as something to be kept on one side and relegated to as limited and narrow a field as possible so that it remains completely fenced off, with no real influence on the rest of existence; are there many Catholics today whose way of thinking and acting in everyday life differs noticeably from that of the most non-religious of their contemporaries? We allude also to the almost complete ignorance of doctrine, and even indifference to everything connected with it; religion, for many, is simply a matter of performance and custom, not to say of routine, and there is a deliberate refusal to attempt to understand anything about it, a refusal that even reaches the point of thinking that it is impossible to understand it, or perhaps that there is nothing there to be understood; moreover, if one really understood religion, could one accord it such a mediocre place among one's preoccupations? Thus, doctrine is in fact forgotten or reduced to almost nothing, which gets close to the Protestant conception, since it is an effect of the same modern tendencies, which are opposed to all intellectuality; and, what is even more deplorable, the teaching commonly given, instead of reacting against this state of mind, favors it by adapting to it only too well: there is constant talk of morality, while very little is said about doctrine, on the pretext that this would not be understood; religion has now become mere moralism, or at least it seems as if nobody cares any longer to see what it really is—and this is something different. And even if doctrine still sometimes comes under discussion, it is too often only diminished by discussing it with its adversaries on their own 'profane' ground, which inevitably leads to making completely unjustifiable concessions. A striking instance is the necessity that people feel to take into consideration, to a greater or less extent, the results claimed by modern 'criticism', whereas, if they were to adopt a different standpoint, nothing would be easier than to show how foolish this is; under such conditions, how can anything remain of the true traditional spirit?

The digression into which we have been led by our review of the manifestations of individualism in the religious field does not seem unjustified, for it shows that the evil, in this domain, is even more serious and widespread than might at first sight be supposed; moreover, it is not really foreign to the question we are considering, upon which our last remark directly bears, for it is individualism that everywhere sponsors the spirit of debate. It is very difficult to make our contemporaries see that there are things which by their very nature cannot be discussed. Modern man, instead of attempting to raise himself to truth, seeks to drag truth down to his own level, which is doubtless the reason why there are so many who imagine, when one speaks to them of 'traditional sciences', or even of pure metaphysics, that one is speaking only of 'profane science' and of 'philosophy'. It is always possible to hold discussions within the realm of individual opinion, as this does not go beyond the rational order, and it is easy to find more or less valid arguments on both sides of a question when there is no appeal to any higher principle. Indeed, in many cases, discussion can be carried on indefinitely without arriving at any solution, which is the reason why almost all modern philosophy is built up on quibbles and badly-framed questions. Far from clearing up these questions, as it is commonly supposed to do, discussion usually only entangles or obscures them still further, and its commonest result is for each participant, in trying to convert his opponent, to become more firmly wedded to his own opinion, and to enclose himself in it more exclusively than ever. The real motive is not the wish to attain to knowledge of the truth, but to prove oneself right in spite of opposition, or at least, if one cannot convince others, to convince oneself of one's own rightness—though failure to convince others nevertheless causes regret, in view of the craving for 'proselytism' that is one of the characteristic features of the modern Western mentality. Sometimes individualism, in the lowest and most vulgar sense of the word, is manifested in a still more obvious way, as in the desire that is frequently shown to judge a man's work by what is known of his private life, as though there could be any sort of connection between the two. The same tendency, combined with a mania for detail, is also responsible for the interest shown in the smallest peculiarities in the lives of 'great men' and for the illusion that all that they have done can be explained by a sort of 'psycho-physiological' analysis; all this is very significant for anyone who wishes to understand the real nature of the contemporary mentality.

To return for a moment to the habit of introducing discussion into realms in which it has no rightful place, it must be stated clearly that an 'apologetic' attitude is in itself extremely weak, because it is merely 'defensive' in the juridical sense of the word; it is not without reason that it is expressed by a word derived from 'apology', the real meaning of which is the plea of an advocate, and which, in English, has even taken on in current usage the meaning of 'excuse'; the excessive importance attached to 'apologetics' is therefore an undeniable proof of the decline of the religious spirit. This weakness becomes still greater when apologetics degenerate, as we remarked above, into discussions—as completely 'profane' in their method as in their point of view—in which religion is put on the same plane as the most contingent and hypothetical of philosophic, scientific, or pseudo-scientific theories, and in which, in order to appear 'conciliatory', the apologists go to the length of admitting, to some extent, conceptions invented for the sole purpose of ruining all religion; such apologists themselves furnish the proof of their complete ignorance of the real character of the doctrine whose more or less authorized representatives they believe themselves to be. Those who are qualified to speak in the name of a traditional doctrine do not need to discuss with the 'profane' or to engage in polemics; they have only to expound the doctrine as it is, for such as can understand it, and, at the same time, to denounce error wherever it arises, and expose it by casting upon it the light of true knowledge. Their function is not to compromise doctrine by taking part in strife, but to pronounce the judgement which they have the right to pronounce, if they effectively possess the principles that should infallibly inspire them. The domain of strife is the domain of action, that is to say the individual and temporal domain; the 'unmoved mover' produces and directs movement without being involved in it; knowledge enlightens action without partaking of its vicissitudes; the spiritual guides the temporal without mingling with it; and thus everything remains in its proper order, in the rank that is its own in the universal hierarchy; but where is the notion of a real hierarchy still to be found in the modern world? Nothing and nobody is any longer in the right place; men no longer recognize any effective authority in the spiritual order or any legitimate power in the temporal; the 'profane' presume to discuss what is sacred, and to contest its character and even its existence; the inferior judges the superior, ignorance sets bounds to wisdom, error prevails over truth, the human is substituted for the Divine, earth has priority over Heaven, the individual sets the measure for all things and claims to dictate to the universe laws drawn entirely from his own relative and fallible reason. 'Woe unto you, ye blind guides,' the Gospel says; and indeed everywhere today one sees nothing but blind leaders of the blind, who, unless restrained by some timely check, will inevitably lead them into the abyss, there to perish with them.

6

THE SOCIAL
CHAOS

IN THE PRESENT WORK, we do not intend to give any particular emphasis to the social point of view, for it interests us only indirectly, representing as it does a comparatively remote application of fundamental principles; it therefore cannot in any circumstances be the domain in which any reconstitution of the modern world could begin. Indeed, if a reconstitution were to be attempted at this level—that is to say, working backward and starting from consequences rather than from principles—it would be bound to lack any real foundation and would be completely illusory. Nothing stable could ever come of it, and the whole work would have to be begun anew because the prime necessity of coming to an agreement on essential truths would have been overlooked. It is for this reason that we find it impossible to consider political contingencies, even in the widest sense of this term, as being more than outward signs of the mentality of a period; but even though we regard them in this light, we cannot altogether overlook the manifestations of the modern confusion as they affect the social sphere.

As we have already pointed out, under the present state of affairs in the Western world, nobody any longer occupies the place that he should normally occupy by virtue of his own nature; this is what is meant by saying that the castes no longer exist, for caste, in its traditional meaning, is nothing other than individual nature, with the whole array of special aptitudes that this carries with it and that predisposes each man to the fulfillment of one or another particular function. Since the undertaking of a function, no matter of what sort, is no longer dictated by any legitimate rule, the inevitable result is that each person finds himself obliged to do whatever kind of work he can get, often that for which he is the least qualified. The part he plays in the community is determined, not by chance—which does not in reality exist[1]—but by what might appear to be chance, that is, by a network of all sorts of incidental circumstances: what exerts the least influence is precisely the one factor that should count for most in the matter, namely the differences of nature between one man and another. It is the negation of these differnces, bringing with it the negation of all social hierarchy, that is the cause of the whole disorder; this negation may not have been deliberate at first, and may have been more practical than theoretical, since the mingling of the castes preceded their complete suppression or, to put it differently, the nature of individuals was misunderstood before it began to be altogether ignored; at all events this same negation has subsequently been raised by the moderns to the rank of a pseudo-principle under the name of 'equality'. It would be quite easy to show that equality can nowhere exist, for the simple reason that there cannot be two beings who are at the same time really distinct and completely alike in every respect; and it would be no less easy to bring out all the ridiculous consequences arising out of this fantastical idea, in the name of which men claim to impose a complete uniformity on everyone, in such ways for example as by meting out identical teaching to all, as though all were equally capable of understanding the same things, and as though the same methods for making them understand these things were suitable for all indiscriminately. However, it could well be asked whether it is not a question of 'learning' rather than of 'understanding', that is to say whether memory is not put in the place of intelligence in the modern, purely verbal and 'bookish' conception of education, whose object is only the accumulation of rudimentary and heterogeneous notions, and in which quality is sacrificed entirely to quantity, as happens—for reasons that we shall explain more fully below—

---

1. What men call chance is simply their ignorance of causes; if the statement that something had happened by chance were to mean that it had no cause, it would be a contradiction in terms.

everywhere in the modern world: here again we have dispersion in multiplicity. Much could be added here concerning the evils of 'compulsory education', but on these we cannot dwell, and, in order to keep within the scheme of the present work, we must confine ourselves to remarking incidentally on this particular consequence of the 'egalitarian theories', as being one of those elements of confusion that today are too numerous for it to be possible to enumerate every single one of them.

Naturally, when we encounter ideas such as 'equality' or 'progress', or any other of the 'lay dogmas' that almost all of our contemporaries blindly accept—most of which were first formulated during the eighteenth century—it is impossible for us to admit that they arose spontaneously. They are veritable 'suggestions', in the strictest sense of this word, though they could not of course have had any effect in a society that was not already prepared to receive them; such ideas in themselves have not actually created the mental outlook that is characteristic of modern times, but they have contributed largely to maintaining it and to bringing it to a stage that would doubtless not have been reached without them. If these suggestions were to disappear, the general mentality would come very near to changing direction; and this is why they are so assiduously fostered by all those who have some interest in maintaining the confusion, if not in making it worse, and also why, at a time when it is claimed that everything is open to discussion, they are the only things that may never be discussed. Moreover, it is not easy to judge the degree of sincerity of those who become the propagators of such ideas, or to know to what extent they fall prey to their own lies and deceive themselves as they deceive others; in fact, in propaganda of this sort, those who play the part of dupes are often the best instruments, as they bring to the work a conviction that others would have difficulty in simulating, and which is readily contagious. But behind all this, at least at the outset, a much more deliberate kind of action is necessary, and the direction can be set only by men fully cognizant of the real nature of the ideas they are spreading. We say 'ideas', but it is only very inexactly that this word can be made to apply in the present case, for it is clear that they are by no means 'pure ideas', having absolutely nothing in common with the intellectual order;

they are rather 'false ideas', though it would be still better to call them 'pseudo-ideas', intended primarily to evoke sentimental reactions, since this is in fact the easiest and most effective way of working on the masses. Indeed, for this purpose, the word used is more important than the notion it is supposed to represent, and most of the modern 'idols' are really mere words, for a remarkable phenomenon has arisen known as 'verbalism', by which sonorous words succeed in creating the illusion of thought; the influence that orators have over the crowd is particularly characteristic in this connection, and it does not require much reflection to see that it is a process of suggestion altogether comparable to that used by hypnotists.

However, without dwelling any longer on these points, let us return to the consequences involved by the negation of all true hierarchy; it must be noticed that not merely does a man, in the present state of affairs, fulfill his proper function only in exceptional cases and as though by accident—his not doing so being the exception—but it also happens that the same man is called upon to fulfill successively completely different functions, as though he could change his aptitudes at will. This may seem paradoxical in an age of extreme 'specialization', and yet it is in fact the case, especially in the realm of politics.

If the competence of specialists is often quite illusory, and in any case limited to a very narrow field, the belief in this competence is nevertheless a fact, and it may well be asked why it is that this belief is not made to apply to the careers of politicians and why, with them, the most complete incompetence is seldom an obstacle. A little reflection, however, will show that there is nothing surprising in this, and that it is in fact a very natural outcome of the democratic conception, according to which power comes from below and is based essentially on the majority, for a necessary corollary of this conception is the exclusion of all real competence, which is always at least a relative superiority, and therefore belongs necessarily to a minority.

Some explanation may be useful here to bring out, on the one hand, the sophistries underlying the democratic idea and, on the other, to show the connection between this idea and the modern mental outlook as a whole. It need hardly be added, considering the point of view at which we place ourself, that these observations will remain entirely aloof from all party questions and all political quarrels, with which we will have nothing whatsoever to do. We regard these matters in an absolutely disinterested way, just as we would any other subject of study, and wish only to bring out as clearly as possible what lies behind them; to do this is indeed necessary—in fact the one thing necessary—if all the illusions that our contemporaries harbor on this subject are to be dispelled. Here too it is really a question of 'suggestion', as it was with the somewhat different but nevertheless kindred ideas of which we have just spoken; and as soon as something is recognized as a suggestion, and its way of working perceived, it can exert no further influence on people's minds; in dealing with things of this sort, a closer and purely 'objective' scrutiny is much more effective than all the sentimental declamations and party controversies that prove nothing and are no more than an expression of individual preferences.

The most decisive argument against democracy can be summed up in a few words: the higher cannot proceed from the lower, because the greater cannot proceed from the lesser; this is an absolute mathematical certainty that nothing can gainsay. And it should be remarked that this same argument, applied to a different order of things, can also be invoked against materialism; there is nothing fortuitous in this, for these two attitudes are much more closely linked than might at first sight appear. It is abundantly clear that the people cannot confer a power that they do not themselves possess; true power can only come from above, and this is why—be it said in passing—it can be legitimized only by the sanction of something standing above the social order, that is to say by a spiritual authority, for otherwise it is a mere counterfeit of power, unjustifiable through lack of any principle, and in which there can be nothing but disorder and confusion. This reversal of the true hierarchical order begins when the temporal power seeks to make itself independent of the spiritual authority, and then even to subordinate the latter by claiming to make it serve political ends. This is an initial usurpation that opens up the way to all the others; thus it could be shown, for example, that the French monarchy was itself working unconsciously, from the fourteenth century onward, to prepare the

Revolution that was to overthrow it; it may be that we shall have the opportunity some day to expound this point of view adequately, but for the moment we can only refer briefly to it in passing.[2]

If the word 'democracy' is defined as the government of the people by themselves, it expresses an absolute impossibility and cannot even have a mere *de facto* existence—in our time or in any other. One must guard against being misled by words: it is contradictory to say that the same persons can be at the same time rulers and ruled, because, to use Aristotelian terminology, the same being cannot be 'in act' and 'in potency' at the same time and in the same relationship. The relationship of ruler and ruled necessitates the presence of two terms: there can be no ruled if there are not also rulers, even though these be illegitimate and have no other title to power than their own pretensions; but the great ability of those who are in control in the modern world lies in making the people believe that they are governing themselves; and the people are the more inclined to believe this as they are flattered by it, and as, in any case, they are incapable of sufficient reflection to see its impossibility. It was to create this illusion that 'universal suffrage' was invented: the law is supposed to be made by the opinion of the majority, but what is overlooked is that this opinion is something that can very easily be guided and modified; it is always possible, by means of suitable suggestions, to arouse, as may be desired, currents moving in this or that direction. We cannot recall who it was who first spoke of 'manufacturing opinion', but this expression is very apt, although it must be added that it is not always those who are in apparent control who really have the necessary means at their disposal. This last remark should make it clear why it is that the incompetence of most prominent politicians seems to have only a very relative importance; but since we are not undertaking here to unmask the working of what might be called the 'machine of government', we will do no more than point out that this incompetence itself serves the purpose of keeping up the illusion of which we have been speaking: indeed, it is a necessary condition if the politicians in question are to appear to issue from the majority, for it makes them in its likeness, inasmuch

2. Guénon did develop these points later in his *Spiritual Authority and Temporal Power*. ED.

as the majority, on whatever question it may be called on to give its opinion, is always composed of the incompetent, whose number is vastly greater than that of the men who can give an opinion based on full knowledge.

This now leads us to elucidate more precisely the error of the idea that the majority should make the law, because, even though this idea must remain theoretical—since it does not correspond to an effective reality—it is necessary to explain how it has taken root in the modern outlook, to which of its tendencies it corresponds, and which of them—at least in appearance—it satisfies. Its most obvious flaw is the one we have just mentioned: the opinion of the majority cannot be anything but an expression of incompetence, whether this be due to lack of intelligence or to ignorance pure and simple; certain observations of 'mass psychology' might be quoted here, in particular the widely known fact that the aggregate of mental reactions aroused among the component individuals of a crowd crystallizes into a sort of general psychosis whose level is not merely not that of the average, but actually that of the lowest elements present. It should also be noted, though in a slightly different connection, that some modern philosophers have even tried to introduce the democratic theory, according to which the opinion of the majority should prevail, into the intellectual realm itself, principally by claiming to find a 'criterion of truth' in what they call 'universal consent'. Even supposing there were some question upon which all men were in agreement, this agreement would prove nothing in itself; moreover, even if such a unanimity really existed—which is all the more unlikely in that, whatever be the question, there are always many people who have no opinion at all and have never even thought about it—it would in any case be impossible to prove it in practice, so that what is invoked in support of an opinion and as a sign of its truth amounts merely to the consent of the majority—the majority of a group moreover that is necessarily very limited in space and time. In this domain the bankruptcy of the theory is even more obvious since it is easier to remove from it the influence of sentiment, which almost inevitably comes into play in the field of politics. It is this influence that is one of the chief obstacles in the way of understanding certain things, even for those who in themselves possess an intellectual capacity sufficient to understand them without difficulty; emotional impulses hinder reflection, and making use of this incompatibility is one of the dishonest tricks practiced in politics.

But let us probe still more deeply into the question: what is this law of the greatest number which modern governments invoke and in which they claim to find their sole justification? It is simply the law of matter and brute force, the same law by which a mass, carried down by its weight, crushes everything that lies in its track. It is precisely here that we find the point of junction of the democratic conception and materialism, and here also is to be found the reason why this conception is so firmly rooted in the present-day mentality. By this means, the normal order of things is completely reversed and the supremacy of multiplicity as such is upheld, a supremacy that actually exists only in the material world;[3] in the spiritual world on the other hand—and more clearly still in the universal order—it is unity that is at the summit of the hierarchy, since unity is the principle out of which all multiplicity arises.[4] Once let the principle be denied or lost from sight and nothing remains but multiplicity pure and simple, which is the same thing as matter. Furthermore, the allusion to weight that we have just made has more significance than that of a mere comparison, for in the field of physical forces—in the commonest meaning of the word—weight effectively represents the downward and compressive tendency, which involves an ever increasing limitation of the being, and at the same time makes for multiplicity, represented here by ever greater density:[5] this tendency has been shaping the development of human activity since the beginning of modern times. It should also be noted that matter,

---

3. One has only to read Saint Thomas Aquinas to see that *numerus stat ex parte materiae* (number is on matter's side).

4. In this case, as in all others, the analogy between one order of reality and another applies in a strictly inverse sense.

5. This tendency is the one that the Hindu doctrine calls *tamas* and assimilates to ignorance and darkness. From what we have just said about the inverse application of all analogy, it will be seen that the compression or condensation in question is directly opposed to concentration of the spiritual or intellectual order, so much so that it is in reality correlative with division and dispersion in multiplicity, however strange this may appear at first sight. The same applies to uniformity obtained, according to the egalitarian conception, from below and at the lowest level, which is the direct opposite of the higher and principial unity.

owing to its power of both dividing and limiting, is what scholastic philosophy calls 'the principle of individuation'. This establishes a connection between the questions we are dealing with now and our earlier remarks about individualism: the tendency of which we have just spoken is identical with that 'individualizing' tendency that is represented in the Judeo-Christian tradition as the 'Fall' of those who broke away from original unity.[6] Multiplicity, considered apart from its principle, and therefore as no longer capable of being reduced to unity, takes the form in the social realm of a community conceived only as the arithmetical sum of its component individuals; in fact, a community is no more than this, once it has ceased to be attached to any principle superior to these individuals. The law of such a community is literally that of the greatest number, and it is on this that the democratic idea is based.

We must pause here to clear up a possible misunderstanding: in speaking of modern individualism we have considered almost exclusively its manifestations in the intellectual order, and it might be supposed that, in the case of the social order, matters might be quite different. Indeed, if one takes the word 'individualism' in its narrowest sense, one could be tempted to oppose the collectivity to the individual, and to think that facts such as the increasingly invasive role of the State and the growing complexity of social institutions indicate a tendency contrary to individualism. In reality however it is not so, because the collectivity, being nothing other than the sum of the individuals within it, cannot be opposed to them, any more than can the State itself, conceived in the modern fashion, and viewed as a simple representation of the masses—in which no higher principle is reflected; and it will be recalled that individualism, as we have defined it, consists precisely in the negation of every supra-individual principle. Therefore, if conflicts arise in the social sphere between tendencies, all of which equally find their place within the modern outlook, they are not conflicts between individualism and something else, but simply between the

---

6. This is why Dante puts the symbolical abode of Lucifer at the center of the earth, that is to say at the point where the forces of weight converge from all sides; from this point of view it is the opposite of the spiritual or 'heavenly' center of attraction symbolized in most traditional doctrines by the sun.

various forms that individualism itself is capable of assuming; it is easy to see that such conflicts must be more numerous and more serious in our time than they have ever been before, owing to the absence of any principle capable of unifying the multiplicity, and because individualism necessarily implies division. This division, with the chaotic state of things resulting from it, is the fatal outcome of an utterly material civilization, for it is matter itself that is really the source of division and multiplicity.

Finally, there remains one direct consequence of the democratic idea to consider, and this is the negation of the idea of an elite; it is not for nothing that 'democracy' is opposed to 'aristocracy', for this latter word, at least when taken in its etymological sense, means precisely the power of the elite. The elite can by definition only be the few, and their power, or rather their authority, deriving as it does from their intellectual superiority, has nothing in common with the numerical strength on which democracy is based, a strength whose inherent tendency is to sacrifice the minority to the majority, and therefore quality to quantity, and the elite to the masses. Thus the guiding function exercised by a true elite, and its very existence—since of necessity it plays this role if it exists at all—is utterly incompatible with democracy, which is closely bound up with the egalitarian conception, and therefore with the negation of all hierarchy; the very foundation of the democratic idea is the supposition that one individual is as good as another, simply because they are equal numerically and in spite of the fact that they can never be equal in any other way. A true elite, as we have already said, can only be an intellectual one; and that is why democracy can arise only where pure intellectuality no longer exists, as is the case in the modern world. However, since equality is in fact impossible, and since, despite all efforts toward leveling, the differences between one man and another cannot in practice be entirely suppressed, men have been brought, by a curious illogic, to invent false elites—of several kinds moreover—that claim to take the place of the one true elite; and these false elites are based on a variety of totally relative and contingent points of superiority, always of a purely material order. This is obvious from the fact that the social distinction that counts most in the present state of things is that based on wealth, that is to say on a purely outward superiority of an exclusively quantitative order, the only superiority in fact that is consistent with democracy, based as it is on the same point of view. It may also be added that even those who set themselves up as opponents of this state of affairs are incapable of producing any real remedy for the disorder, and may even aggravate it by going ever further in the same direction, because they also make no appeal to any principle of a higher order. The struggle is merely between different varieties of democracy, with more or less emphasis on the egalitarian tendency, just as it is, as we have said above, a struggle between the varieties of individualism, which amounts to exactly the same thing.

These few reflections seem sufficient to give an idea of the social conditions of the contemporary world and, at the same time, to show that there can be only one way out of the chaos, in the social domain as in all others: the restoration of intellectuality, which would result in the formation once more of an elite. This elite must be regarded as presently non-existent in the West, since the name cannot be applied to the few isolated and disconnected elements that do no more than represent, so to speak, non-developed possibilities. Indeed, these elements usually show little more than tendencies or aspirations, which lead them, it is true, to react against the modern outlook, but without their being able to influence it in any effective way. What they lack is true knowledge and traditional data, which cannot be improvised and which an intelligence left to its own resources—especially in circumstances so unfavorable in every respect—can only supply imperfectly and to a very slight extent. Consequently, there are nothing but disjointed efforts, which often go astray owing to lack of principle and doctrinal guidance; it might be said that the modern world protects itself by its very dispersion, from which even its adversaries do not succeed in escaping. This will continue to be the case as long as the latter keep to the 'profane' ground on which the modern mentality enjoys an obvious advantage, as this is its proper and exclusive province; and, as a matter of fact, their remaining on this ground shows that, despite all appearances, this mentality still has a very strong hold over them. It is for this reason that so many people, although moved by undeniably good intentions, are unable to understand that a beginning can be made only from principles, and persist in frittering away their energies in some relative sphere, social or otherwise, in which, under such conditions, nothing real or durable can ever be accomplished. The true elite, on the other hand, would not have to intervene directly in these spheres, or take any part in outward action; it would direct everything by an influence of which the people were unaware, and which, the less visible it was, the more powerful it would be. It is enough to consider the already mentioned power of suggestion, which does not demand any true intellectuality, in order to get an idea of how much greater would be the power of an influence that was based on pure intellectuality, and worked even more invisibly because of its very nature. Instead of this power being lessened by the division inherent in multiplicity, and by the weakness involved by all lies and illusions, it would on the contrary be intensified by concentration on principial unity, and would be one with the strength of truth itself.

7

A MATERIAL
CIVILIZATION

FROM ALL THAT HAS BEEN SAID ABOVE, it seems sufficiently clear that Easterners are justified in reproaching modern Western civilization for being exclusively material: it has developed along purely material lines only, and from whatever point of view it is considered, one is faced with the more or less direct results of this materialization. However, there is still something to be added to what we have already said about this: in the first place, we must explain the different meanings that can be given to a word such as 'materialism', for if we use it to characterize the contemporary world, people who claim to be very modern, without considering themselves in any way materialistic, will be sure to protest and will feel convinced that this is mere calumny; we must therefore begin with an explanation that will remove in advance any ambiguity that might arise on this point.

It is significant in itself that the very word 'materialism' does not go any further back than the eighteenth century; it was invented by the philosopher Berkeley, who used it to designate any theory that accepted the real existence of matter; it is scarcely necessary to say that it is not this meaning of the word that concerns us here, since we are not raising the question of the existence of matter. A little later the same word took on a narrower meaning, the one in fact that it still retains: it came to denote a conception according to which nothing else exists but matter and its derivatives. It should be remarked that such a conception is something altogether new and essentially a product of the modern outlook, and therefore corresponds to at least some of the tendencies that are inherent in this outlook.[1] But we intend at present to speak of materialism mainly in another, much wider, and yet very definite sense: in this sense, materialism stands for a complete state of mind, of which the conception that we have just described is only one manifestation among many others, and which, in itself, is independent of any philosophical theory. This state of mind is one that consists in more or less consciously putting material things, and the preoccupations arising out of them, in the first place, whether these preoccupations claim to be speculative or purely practical; and it cannot be seriously disputed that this is the mentality of the immense majority of our contemporaries. The whole of the 'profane' science that has developed in the course of recent centuries is a study of only the sensible world, is enclosed entirely within this world, and works by methods that can be applied only to this domain; these methods alone are proclaimed to be 'scientific', which amounts to rejecting any science that does not deal with material things. Among those who think in this way, and even among those who have specialized in the sciences in question, there are nevertheless many who would refuse to call themselves materialists, or accept the philosophical theory that bears this name. There are even some who gladly profess a religious faith, and whose sincerity is not in doubt; but their scientific attitude does not differ appreciably from that of the avowed materialists. The question has often been raised whether, from the religious point of view, modern science should be denounced as atheistic or materialistic, but the question has usually been badly put: it is quite certain that this science does not explicitly profess atheism or materialism, it merely, because of its prejudices, ignores certain things, without formally denying them, as this or that philosopher may have done; in connection with modern science, therefore, one can only speak of *de facto* materialism, or what might be called practical materialism; but the evil is perhaps even more serious, as it is deeper and more widespread. A philosophical attitude

---

1. Prior to the eighteenth century there were 'mechanistic' theories, from Greek atomism down to Cartesian physics, but mechanism should not be confused with materialism, despite certain affinities that may have subsequently brought about a kind of fellowship between them.

may be something very superficial, even with the 'professional' philosophers; and besides, there are people whose mind would recoil from actual negation, but who have no objection to complete indifference; this is what is most to be feared, for to deny something one must think about it to some extent, however little that may be, whereas an attitude of indifference makes it possible not to think about it at all. When an exclusively material science claims to be the only science possible, and when men are accustomed to accept, as an unquestionable truth, that there can be no valid knowledge outside this science, and when all the education they receive tends to instill into them the superstition of this science—or 'scientism' as it should really be called—how could these men not in fact be materialists, or in other words, how could they fail to have all their preoccupations turned in the direction of matter?

It seems that nothing exists for modern men beyond what can be seen and touched; or at least, even if they admit theoretically that something more may exist, they immediately declare it not merely unknown but unknowable, which absolves them from having to think about it. There are, it is true, people who try to create for themselves some idea of an 'other world' but, relying as they do on nothing but their imagination, they represent it in the likeness of the terrestrial world, and endow it with all the conditions of existence that belong to this world, including space and time and even a sort of 'corporeality'; we have shown elsewhere, in speaking of spiritist[2] conceptions, some particularly striking examples of this kind of grossly materialized representation. But if these conceptions represent an extreme case, in which this trait is exaggerated to the point of caricature, it would be wrong to suppose that this sort of thing is confined to spiritism and to the sects that are more or less akin to it. Indeed, in a more general manner, the intrusion of the imagination into realms in which it can be of no service, and which should normally be closed to it, shows very clearly the inability of modern Westerners to rise above the sensible domain. There are many who can see no difference between 'conceiving' and 'imagining', and

---

2. For a detailed exposition of 'spiritism', see the author's *The Spiritist Fallacy*. ED.

some philosophers—such as Kant—have gone so far as to declare 'inconceivable' or 'unthinkable' everything that is not susceptible of representation. Likewise, what is called 'spiritualism' or 'idealism' is usually only a sort of transposed materialism; and this is true not only of what we have termed 'neo-spiritualism', but also of philosophical spiritualism itself, even though this holds itself to be the opposite of materialism. Indeed spiritualism and materialism, in the philosophical sense of these words, cannot be understood apart from each other, being merely the two halves of the Cartesian dualism, whose radical separation has been transformed into a sort of antagonism; since that time, the whole of philosophy has oscillated between these two terms, without being able to get beyond them. Despite its name, spiritualism has nothing in common with spirituality; its war with materialism cannot be of the slightest interest to those who adopt a higher point of view, and who see that these two alleged opposites are basically close to being simple equivalents, and that on many points their pretended opposition ultimately amounts to no more than a mere verbal dispute.

Modern persons in general cannot conceive of any other science than that of things that can be measured, counted, and weighed, in other words material things, since it is to these alone that the quantitative point of view can be applied; the claim to reduce quality to quantity is very typical of modern science. This tendency has reached the point of supposing that there can be no science, in the real meaning of the word, except where it is possible to introduce measurement, and that there can be no scientific laws except those that express quantitative relations. It is a tendency that arose with the mechanism of Descartes; since then it has become more and more pronounced, notwithstanding the rejection of Cartesian physics, for it is not bound up with any particular physical theory, but with a general conception of scientific knowledge. Today, attempts are made to apply measurement even in the psychological field, the very nature of which excludes such a method. The point has been reached of no longer understanding that the possibility of measurement derives from a quality inherent in matter, that is to say from its indefinite divisibility; or else it is thought that this quality is to be found in all that exists, which comes to the same as materializing everything. As we have said before, matter is the principle of division and of all that is multiplicity; the predominance given to the quantitative point of view—a predominance to be found, as we have already shown, even in the social domain—is thus really materialism in the sense that we defined above; this materialism is not necessarily connected with philosophical materialism, which, in fact, it preceded in the development of the tendencies inherent in the modern outlook. We will not dwell on the mistake of seeking to reduce quality to quantity, or on the inadequacy of all attempts at explanation that are more or less of the 'mechanistic' type. That is not our present purpose, and we will remark only, in this connection, that even in the sensible order, a science of this kind has but little connection with reality, the greater part of which is bound to elude it.

Speaking of 'reality' leads us to mention another fact, which might easily be overlooked, but which is very significant as a sign of the state of mind we are speaking of: it is that people commonly use the word 'reality' to denote exclusively reality of the sensible order. As language expresses the mentality of a people or a period, one must conclude that, for such people, everything that cannot be grasped by the senses is 'unreal', that is to say illusory or even non-existent. They may not be clearly aware of it, but this negative conviction is nonetheless deeply held and, if they deny it, one can be certain that though they may not be aware of it their denial is merely the expression of something even more outward, and indeed may be no more than verbal. If anyone should be tempted to think that we are exaggerating, he has only to consider, for example, what the so-called religious convictions of many people amount to, namely a few notions learnt by heart, in a purely mechanical and schoolboy way, which they have never assimilated, to which they have never devoted serious thought, but which they store in their memory and repeat on occasion as part of a certain convention or formal attitude which is all they understand by the name of religion. We have already spoken of this 'minimization' of religion, of which the 'verbalism' in question represents one of the final stages, and it is this that explains why so-called 'believers' in no wise fall short of 'unbelievers' as regards practical materialism. We shall return to this point later, but first we must complete our description of the materialistic character of modern science, for this is a subject that requires to be treated from various angles.

We must recall once more a point that has already been mentioned: modern sciences do not possess the character of disinterested knowledge, nor is their speculative value, even for those who believe in it, much more than a mask beneath which purely practical considerations are hidden; but this mask makes it possible to retain the illusion of a false intellectuality. Descartes himself, in working out his physics, was primarily interested in extracting from it a system of mechanics, medicine, and morality; but a still greater change was brought about by the diffusion of the influence of Anglo-Saxon empiricism. It is almost exclusively the practical results that science makes possible that gives it so much prestige in the eyes of the general public, because here again are things that can be seen and touched. We have said that pragmatism represents the outcome of all modern philosophy, and the last stage in its decline; but outside philosophy there is also, and has been for a long time, a widespread and unsystematized pragmatism that is to philosophical pragmatism what practical is to theoretical materialism, and which is really the same as what people call 'common sense'. What is more, this almost instinctive utilitarianism is inseparable from the materialist tendency, for, 'common sense' consists in not going beyond the things of this earth, as well as in ignoring all that does not make an immediate practical appeal. In particular, it is 'common sense' that sees only the world of the senses as real, and that admits of no knowledge other than the one that comes from the senses; moreover, it ascribes value to this narrow form of knowledge only insofar as it offers a possibility of satisfying either material needs or a certain sentimentalism, for in reality sentiment—and this must be frankly stated at the risk of shocking contemporary moralism—lies quite close to matter. In all this there remains no place for intelligence, or at most only insofar as intelligence may consent to serve for the attainment of practical ends, and to become a mere instrument subordinated to the requirements of the lowest and most corporeal part of the human individual—'a tool for making tools', to quote a significant expression of Bergson: it is an utter indifference to truth that begets pragmatism in all its forms.

Under such conditions, industry is no longer merely an application of science, an application from which science should, in itself, remain completely independent; it has become the reason for, and justification of, science to such an extent that here too the normal relations between things have been reversed. What the modern world has striven after with all its strength, even when it has claimed in its own way to pursue science, is really nothing other than the development of industry and machinery; and in thus seeking to dominate matter and bend it to their service, men have only succeeded, as we said at the beginning of this book, in becoming its slaves. Not only have they limited their intellectual ambition—if such a term can still be used in the present state of things—to inventing and constructing machines, but they have ended by becoming in fact machines themselves. Indeed, it is not only scholars but also technicians and even workers who have to undergo the specialization that certain sociologists praise so highly under the name of 'division of labor'; and for the 'workers', it makes intelligent work quite impossible. Very different from the craftsmen of former times, they have become mere slaves of machines with which they may be said to form part of a single body. In a purely mechanical way they have constantly to repeat certain specific movements, which are always the same and always performed in the same way, so as to avoid the slightest loss of time; such at least is required by the most modern methods which are supposed to represent the most advanced stage of 'progress'. Indeed, the object is merely to produce as much as possible; quality matters little, it is quantity alone that is of importance, which brings us back once more to the remark we have already made in other contexts, namely, that modern civilization may truly be called a quantitative civilization, and this is merely another way of saying it is a material civilization.

Anyone who wants still further evidence of this truth can find it in the tremendous importance that economic factors take on nowadays, both in the lives of peoples and of individuals: industry, commerce, finance—these seem to be the only things that count; and this is in agreement with the fact already mentioned that the only social distinction that has survived is the one based on material wealth. Politics seem to be altogether controlled by finance, and trade competition seems to be the dominant influence in determining the relations between peoples; it may be that this is only so in appearance, and that these factors are really not so much causes as means of action, but the choice of such means is a clear sign of the character of the period to which they are suited. Moreover, our contemporaries are convinced that it is almost exclusively economic conditions that dictate historical events, and they even imagine that it has always been so; a theory has even been invented according to which everything is to be explained by economic factors alone, and has been named, significantly, 'historical materialism'. Here also may be seen the effect of one of those suggestions to which we referred above, suggestions whose power is all the greater in that they correspond to the tendencies of the general mentality; and the result of this suggestion is that economic factors have really come to decide almost everything that occurs in the social sphere. It is true that the masses have always been led in one manner or another, and it could be said that their part in history consists primarily in allowing themselves to be led, since they represent a merely passive element, a 'matter' in the Aristotelian sense of the word. But, in order to lead them today, it is sufficient to dispose of purely material means, this time in the ordinary sense of the word, and this shows clearly to what depths our age has sunk. At the same time, the masses are made to believe that they are not being led, but that they are acting spontaneously and governing themselves, and the fact that they believe this is a sign from which the extent of their stupidity may be inferred.

As we are speaking of economic factors, we will take the opportunity to mention a widespread illusion on this subject, namely that of supposing that relations established in the field of commerce can serve to draw peoples closer together and bring about an understanding between them, whereas in reality they have exactly the opposite effect. Matter, as we have often pointed out, is essentially multiplicity and division, and therefore the source of struggles and conflicts; also, whether with peoples or individuals, the economic field is and can only be that of rival interests. In particular, the West cannot count on industry, any more than on the modern science that is inseparable from it, to serve as a basis for an understanding with the East; if Easterners bring themselves to accept this industry as an unpleasant and transitory necessity, it will only be as a weapon to enable them to resist the invasion of the West and to safeguard their own existence. It should be clearly understood that this is bound to be so: Easterners who bring themselves to consider economic competition with the West, despite the repugnance they feel for this kind of activity, can do so only with one purpose, namely to rid themselves of a foreign domination that is based on mere brute force, and on the material power that industry itself supplies; violence breeds violence, but it should be recognized that it is certainly not the Easterners who have sought war in this field.

Moreover, apart from the question of the relations between East and West, it is easy to see that one of the most conspicuous results of industrial development is that engines of war are being constantly perfected and their power of destruction increased at an ominous rate. This alone should be enough to shatter the 'pacifist' dreams of some of the admirers of modernist 'progress'; but the dreamers and idealists are incorrigible, and their gullibility seems to know no bounds. The 'humanitarianism' that is so much in fashion is certainly not worth taking seriously; but it is strange that people should talk so much about ending all war at a time when the ravages it causes are greater than they have ever been, not only because the means of destruction have been multiplied, but also because, as wars are no longer fought between comparatively small armies composed solely of professional soldiers, all the individuals on both sides are flung against each other indiscriminately, including those who are the least qualified for this kind of function. Here again is a striking example of modern confusion, and it is truly portentous, for those who care to reflect upon it, that a 'mass uprising' or a 'general mobilization' should have come to be considered quite natural, and that with very few exceptions the minds of all should have accepted the idea of an 'armed nation'. In this also can be seen an outcome of the belief in the power of numbers alone: it is in keeping with the quantitative character of modern civilization to set in motion enormous masses of combatants; and at the same time, egalitarianism also finds its expression here, as well as in systems such as 'compulsory education' and 'universal suffrage'. Let it be added that these generalized wars have only been made possible by another specifically modern phenomenon, that is, by the formation of 'nations'—a consequence on the one hand of the destruction of the feudal system, and on the other of the disruption of the higher unity of medieval Christendom; and, without pausing over considerations that would carry us too far afield, let us point out that matters have been made still worse by the non-recognition of any spiritual authority which, under normal conditions, could be an effective arbiter, standing as it does by its very nature above all conflicts of the political order. Denial of the spiritual authority is the same thing as practical materialism; and even those who in theory claim to recognize such an authority refuse in practice to allow it any real influence or power of intervention in the social domain, in exactly the same way as they fence off religion from the concerns of their every-day existence: whether in public or in private life, it is the same mental outlook that prevails.

Even if we admit that material development does have certain advantages—though, indeed, from a very relative point of view—the sight of consequences such as those just mentioned leads one to question whether they are not far outweighed by the inconveniences. We say this without referring to the many things of incomparably greater value that have been sacrificed to this one form of development—we do not speak of the higher knowledge that has been forgotten, the intellectuality that has been overthrown, and the spirituality that has disappeared. Simply taking modern civilization on its merits, we affirm that, if the advantages and inconveniences of what has been brought about were set against each other, the result might well on balance prove to be negative. The inventions, whose number is at present growing at an ever-increasing pace, are all the more dangerous in that they bring into play forces whose real nature is quite unknown to the men who utilize them; and this ignorance is the best proof of the worthlessness of modern science as an explanatory means, that is to say considered as knowledge, even were one's attention confined entirely to the physical realm. At the same time, the fact that such ignorance in no way interferes with practical applications proves that this science is in reality directed only to practical ends, and that it is industry that is the only real object of all its research. The danger inherent in these inventions, even in those that are not expressly created for a purpose destructive to mankind—but which nonetheless cause just as many catastrophes, without mentioning the unsuspected disturbances that they create in the physical environment—will undoubtedly continue to grow, and that to an extent difficult to foretell, so that, as we have already shown, it is by no means improbable that it will be through these inventions that the modern world will bring about its own destruction, unless it can check its course in this direction while there is still time.

It is not enough however to withhold approval of modern inventions on the grounds of their dangerous side alone; there is more than this to the affair. One hears of the 'benefits' claimed for what men have agreed to call 'progress', and that one might even consent so to call, provided one take care to make it clear that there is no question of any but a purely material progress; but are not these 'benefits', of which people are so proud, very largely illusory? Our contemporaries claim they increase their 'welfare' by this means; in our opinion, the end they set themselves, even if it were really attained, is hardly worth the expenditure of so much effort; but what is more, it seems a very debatable question whether they do attain it. In the first place, the fact should be taken into account that not all men have the same tastes or the same needs, and that there are still some who would wish to avoid modern commotion and the craving for speed, but who can no longer do so. Could anyone presume to maintain that it is a 'benefit' to these people to have thrust on them what is most contrary to their nature? It will be said in reply that there are few such men today, and this is considered a justification for treating them as a negligible quantity; in this, as in the field of politics, the majority arrogates to itself the right to crush minorities, which, in its eyes, evidently have no right to exist, since their very existence defies the egalitarian mania for uniformity. But if the whole of mankind be taken into consideration, instead of merely the Western world, the question bears a different aspect: the majority we have just spoken of then becomes a minority. A different argument is therefore used in this case, and by a strange contradiction it is in the name of their 'superiority' that these 'egalitarians' seek to impose their civilization on the rest of the world, and that they bring trouble to people who have never asked them for anything; and, since this 'superiority' exists only from the material point of view, it is quite natural that the most brutal means are used to assert it. Let there be no confusion on this point: if the general public accepts the pretext of 'civilization' in all good faith, there are those for whom it is no more than mere moralistic hypocrisy, serving as a mask for designs of conquest or economic ambitions. It is really an extraordinary epoch in which so many men can be made to believe that a people is being given happiness by being reduced to subjection, by being robbed of all that is most precious to it, that is to say of its own civilization, by being forced to adopt manners and institutions that were made for a different race, and by being constrained to the most distasteful kinds of work, in order to make it acquire things for which it has not the slightest use. For that is what is taking place: the modern West cannot tolerate that men should prefer to work less and be content to live on little; as it is only quantity that counts, and as everything that escapes the senses is held to be nonexistent, it is taken for granted that anyone who is not in a state of agitation and who does not produce much in a material way must be 'lazy'. In evidence of this and without speaking of the opinions commonly expressed about Eastern peoples, it is enough to note how the contemplative orders are viewed, even in circles that consider themselves religious. In such a world, there is no longer any place for intelligence, or anything else that is purely inward, for these are things that can neither be seen nor touched, that can neither be counted nor weighed; there is a place only for outward action in all its forms, even those that are the most completely meaningless. For this reason it should not be a matter for surprise that the Anglo-Saxon mania for sport gains ground day by day: the ideal of the modern world is the 'human animal' who has developed his muscular strength to the highest pitch; its heroes are athletes, even though they be mere brutes; it is they who awaken popular enthusiasm, and it is their exploits that command the passionate interest of the crowd. A world in which such things are seen has indeed sunk low and seems near its end.

However, let us consider things for a moment from the standpoint of those whose ideal is material 'welfare', and who therefore rejoice at all the improvements to life furnished by modern 'progress'; are they quite sure they are not being duped? Is it true that, because they dispose of swifter means of communication and other things of the kind, and because of their more agitated and complicated manner of life, men are happier today than they were formerly? The very opposite seems to us to be true: disequilibrium cannot be a condition of real happiness. Moreover, the more needs a man has, the greater the likelihood that he will lack something, and thereby be unhappy; modern civilization aims at creating more and more artificial needs, and as we have already said, it will always create more needs than it can satisfy, for once one has started on this path, it is very hard to stop, and, indeed, there is no reason for stopping at any particular point. It was no hardship for men to do without things that did not exist and of which they had never dreamed; now, on the contrary, they are bound to suffer if they lack these things, since they have become accustomed to consider them as necessities, with the result that they have, in fact, really become necessary to them. Therefore men struggle in every possible way to obtain the means of procuring material satisfactions, the only ones that they are capable of appreciating: they are interested only in 'making money', because it is money that enables them to obtain these things, the more of which they have, the more they wish to have, as they go on discovering fresh needs; and this passion becomes for them the sole end in life. Hence the savage competition certain evolutionists have raised to the dignity of a scientific law under the name of 'the struggle for existence', whose logical consequence is that only the strongest, in the narrowly material sense of the word, have a right to exist. Hence also the envy and even hatred felt toward those who possess wealth by those who do not; how could men to whom egalitarian theories have been preached fail to revolt when they see all around them inequality in the most material order of things, the order to which they are bound to be the most sensitive? If modern civilization should some day be destroyed by the disordered appetites that it has awakened in the masses, one would have to be very blind not to see in this the just punishment of its basic vice—or, without resorting to the language of morality, the repercussion of its own action in the same domain in which this action has taken place. The Gospel says 'all they that take the sword shall perish by the sword'; those who unchain the brute forces of matter will perish, crushed by these same forces, of which they will no longer be masters; having once imprudently set them in motion, they cannot hope to hold back indefinitely their fatal course. It is of little consequence whether it be the forces of nature or the forces of the human mob, or both together; in any case it is the laws of matter that are called into play, and that will inexorably destroy him who has aspired to dominate them without raising himself above matter. The Gospel also says: 'If a house be divided against itself, that house cannot stand'; this saying also applies fully to the modern world with its material civilization, which cannot fail, by its very nature, to cause strife and division everywhere. The conclusion is obvious and, even without appealing to other considerations, it is possible to predict with all certainty that this world will come to a tragic end, unless a change as radical as to amount to a complete reversal of direction should intervene, and that very soon.

In speaking as we have done of the materialism of modern civilization, we are aware that some will reproach us for having overlooked certain elements that seem at least to alleviate this materialism; and indeed, if there were none such, one could truly say that this civilization would most probably have already perished miserably. We do not, therefore, in the least dispute that there are such elements, but on the other hand there should be no illusions on this subject: in the first place, the various philosophical movements that assume labels such as 'spiritualism' and 'idealism' are not to be counted among them, any more than are the contemporary tendencies that take the form of moralism and sentimentalism. We have already explained the reasons for this, and wish merely to recall that for us these points of view are no less 'profane' than theoretical or practical materialism, and far less remote from it in reality than in appearance. In the second place, if there are still remnants of real spirituality, it is in spite of the modern outlook and in opposition to it that they have persisted. Such remnants of spirituality, insofar as they are really Western, are to be found only in religion; but we have already remarked how shrunken religion is today, what a narrow and mediocre conception of it even believers hold, and to what point it has been deprived of intellectuality, which is one with true spirituality; under such conditions, if certain possibilities still remain, it is merely in a latent state, and their effective influence amounts to very little. It is nonetheless remarkable to see the vitality of a religious tradition that, even though sunk thus into a sort of virtual state, still endures despite all the attempts made in the course of several centuries to crush and destroy it. Those who are capable of reflection must see in this resistance signs of a more than human power; but we must repeat once more that this tradition does not belong to the modern world, nor is it one of its component elements, but is the direct opposite of its tendencies and aspirations. This should be admitted frankly, instead of seeking for a vain conciliation: there can be nothing but antagonism between the religious spirit, in the true sense of the word, and the modern mentality, and any compromise is bound to weaken the former and favor the latter, whose hostility moreover will not be placated thereby, since it can only aim at the utter destruction of everything that reflects in mankind a reality higher than the human.

The modern West is said to be Christian, but this is untrue: the modern outlook is anti-Christian, because it is essentially anti-religious; and it is anti-religious because, still more generally, it is anti-traditional; this is its distinguishing characteristic and this is what makes it what it is. Undoubtedly, something of Christianity has passed even into the anti-Christian civilization of our time, even the most 'advanced' of whose representatives, to use their own jargon, cannot help, involuntarily and perhaps unconsciously, having undergone and still undergoing a certain Christian influence, though an indirect one; however radical a breach with the past may be, it can never be quite complete and such as to break all continuity. More than this: we even assert that everything of value that there may be in the modern world has come to it from Christianity, or at any rate through Christianity, for Christianity has brought with it the whole heritage of former traditions, has kept this heritage alive so far as the state of things in the West made it possible, and still contains its latent possibilities. But is there anyone today, even among those calling themselves Christians, who has any real consciousness of these possibilities? Where are to be found, even in

Catholicism, the men who know the deeper meaning of the doctrine that they profess outwardly, and who, not content with 'believing' in a more or less superficial way—and more through sentiment than intelligence—really 'know' the truth of the tradition they hold to be theirs? We would wish to see proof that there are at least a few such men, for this would be the greatest and perhaps the sole hope of salvation for the West; but we have to admit that, up to the present, we have not encountered any: is one to suppose that they live in hiding, like certain Eastern sages, in some almost inaccessible retreat, or must this last hope be definitely abandoned? The West was Christian in the Middle Ages, but is so no longer; if anyone should reply that it may again become so, we will rejoinder that no one desires this more than we do, and may it come about sooner than all we see round about us would lead us to expect. But let no one delude himself on this point: if this should happen, the modern world will have lived its day.

8

WESTERN
ENCROACHMENT

THE MODERN CONFUSION had its origin in the West, as we have already said, and until the last few years remained in the West. But now a process is taking place, the gravity of which should not be overlooked: the confusion is spreading everywhere, and even the East seems to be succumbing to it. It is true that the encroachments of the West are nothing new, but hitherto they have been confined to a more or less brutal domination over other peoples, whose effects went no deeper than the domain of politics and economics: despite all the efforts of a propaganda that worked under many different guises, the Eastern attitude of mind remained unaffected by all deviations, and the ancient traditional civilizations survived intact. Today, on the contrary, there are Easterners who are more or less completely 'Westernized', who have forsaken their tradition and adopted all the aberrations of the modern outlook, and these denatured elements—led astray by the teachings of European and American universities—have become a cause of trouble and agitation in their own countries. At the same time, their importance, at least for the moment, should not be exaggerated: Westerners are apt to imagine that these noisy but not very numerous individuals represent the East of today, whereas actually their influence is neither very widespread nor very deep. This mistake is easily explained, since the real Easterners make no effort at all to become known, and are therefore ignored by the West, while the modernists, if one may so call them, are the only ones who thrust themselves forward, make speeches, write, and indulge in all manner of outward activity. It is nonetheless true that this anti-traditional movement may gain ground, and all eventualities, even the most unfavorable, must be considered.

The traditional spirit is already tending as it were to withdraw into itself, and the centers where it is preserved in its entirety are becoming more and more closed and difficult of access; this generalization of confusion corresponds exactly to what must occur in the final phase of the *Kali-Yuga*.

Let it be stated quite clearly: the modern outlook is purely Western, and those who are affected by it should be classed as Westerners mentally, even though they may be Easterners by birth; all Eastern ideas are completely alien to them, and their ignorance of the traditional doctrines is the only excuse for their hostility toward them. What may seem remarkable, and even contradictory, is that these same individuals who become the auxiliaries of 'Westernism' from an intellectual point of view—or, more exactly, in opposition to all real intellectuality—sometimes come to the fore as the opponents of the West in the field of politics. But there is nothing surprising in this, for it is they who strive to introduce the idea of 'nation' in the East, and all nationalism is essentially opposed to the traditional outlook; they may wish to resist foreign domination, but in order to do so they make use of Western methods, such as are used by the various Western peoples when fighting among themselves; and it may be that in this fact lies the justification for their existence. Indeed, if things have reached a point where the employment of such methods is inevitable, the sort of work involved can only be carried out by those elements of the community that have severed all connection with tradition. It is possible therefore that these elements may be temporarily utilized to this end and then eliminated, like the Westerners themselves. Moreover, it would be quite logical for the ideas spread by Westerners to turn against them, since they are of a kind that can never beget anything but division and ruin. It is through these ideas that the modern world will perish in one way or another; it is of small importance whether this be by way of quarrels among Westerners themselves, quarrels between nations, between social classes, or, as some people assert, through the attacks of 'Westernized' Easterners—or, another possibility, as the result of a cataclysm brought about by the 'progress of science'; in any case, the dangers facing the Western world are entirely of its own making and proceed from itself.

The only question to arise is this: will the East, as a result of modern influence, have to undergo a merely transitory and superficial crisis, or will the West involve the whole of mankind in its own downfall? It would be difficult at present to give any answer based on undeniable evidence; both contrary outlooks are now to be found in the East, but the spiritual power inherent in tradition, of which its adversaries know nothing, may triumph over the material power when this has played its part, and disperse it as light disperses the shadows; we may even say that it must triumph sooner or later, but it is possible that there will be a period of complete darkness before this happens. The traditional spirit cannot die, being in its essence above death and change; but it can withdraw completely from the outward world, and then there would really be the 'end of a world'. From all that has been said, one may conclude that such an eventuality in the not far distant future is by no means unlikely; and, in the confusion that has arisen in the West and that is at present over-flowing into the East, we may see the 'beginning of the end', the preliminary sign of the moment when, according to the Hindu tradition, the whole of the sacred doctrine is to be shut in a conch-shell, from which it will once more come forth intact at the dawn of the new world.

But let us cease anticipating and turn to present events: the West is undeniably encroaching everywhere; its influence first made itself felt in the material domain, since this comes most directly within its reach, working through conquest by violence or through commerce, and by securing control over the resources of other countries; but now things are going still further. Westerners, always animated by that need for proselytism which is so exclusively theirs, have succeeded to a certain extent in introducing their own anti-traditional and materialistic outlook among other peoples; and whereas the first form of invasion only affected men's bodies, this newer form poisons their minds and kills all spirituality. In point of fact, it was the first kind of invasion that made the second one possible, so that it is ultimately only by brute force that the West has succeeded in imposing itself upon the rest of the world, as, indeed, must necessarily be the case, since in this sphere alone lies the superiority of its civilization, so inferior from every other point of view.

The Western encroachment is the encroachment of materialism under all its guises and cannot be other than this; none of the more or less hypocritical veils, none of the moralistic pretexts, none of the humanitarian declamations, none of the wiles of a propaganda that knows how to be insinuating the better to achieve its destructive ends, none of these things can gainsay that Western encroachment is the encroachment of materialism; this could be disputed only by the gullible, or by those who have an interest in aiding a process that is truly 'satanic' in the strictest sense of the word.[1]

It is extraordinary that the very moment that Western encroachment is penetrating everywhere is the moment chosen by some people to raise a cry against the peril, dreadful for them, of a supposed infiltration of Eastern ideas into the West; what new aberration can this be? Despite the wish to confine ourselves to considerations of a general order, we cannot avoid saying here a few words about a recently-published book by Henri Massis entitled *Défense de l'Occident*, which is one of the most characteristic manifestations of this frame of mind.[2] It is a book full of confusion and contradiction, and shows once more to what extent most of those who seek to react against the modern disorder are incapable of doing so in a really effective way, since they are not even very clear as to what they are fighting against. The author at times disclaims the intention of attacking the real East; and if he had in fact confined himself to a criticism of 'pseudo-oriental' fantasies, that is to say of purely Western theories that are being spread abroad under deceptive names and that are merely one of the many products of the present disequilibrium, this could only meet with our full approval, especially since we ourself have drawn attention to the real danger of this sort of thing, as well as to its inanity from an intellectual point of view. Unfortunately however, he does not stop there, but feels the need to

1. Satan, in Hebrew, is the 'adversary', the one who 'turns things upside down'; this is the spirit of negation and subversion, which is identical with the descending or 'downward' tendency (*tamas*)—'infernal' in the etymological sense of the word—and which governs beings in this process of materialization, upon which the whole development of modern civilization is based.

2. Henri Massis, *Défence de l'Occident* (Paris: Plon, 1927), translated into English as *Defence of the West* (New York: Harcourt, Brace & Company, 1928). ED.

attribute to the East conceptions scarcely better than these and, to do so, relies upon quotations taken from certain more or less 'official' orientalists, in which the Eastern doctrines are—as usually happens—deformed to the point of caricature. What would he say if somebody were to adopt the same method in dealing with Christianity, and claim to judge it on the basis of the works of the university 'hypercritics'? This is exactly what he does with the doctrines of India and China, with the aggravating circumstance that the Westerners whose testimony he produces have not the slightest direct knowledge of these doctrines, whereas their fellow critics who occupy themselves with Christianity must at least be familiar with it to a certain extent, even if their hostility toward all that has to do with religion prevents them from really understanding it. Moreover, we must add in this connection that we have sometimes found it hard to convince Easterners that the studies of some orientalist or other were the outcome of incomprehension pure and simple, and not of a conscious and deliberate bias, so imbued are these writings with that same hostility that is inherent in the anti-traditional outlook; and we might well ask Massis whether he really considers it advisable to attack tradition abroad while striving to restore it at home. We say 'advisable', because the whole discussion is, for him, really placed within the realm of politics; since we take a different point of view, that of pure intellectuality, the only question that matters to us is that of truth; but such a point of view is doubtless too high and too serene for polemicists to find any satisfaction in it, and it is even doubtful whether, in their capacity as controversialists, the truth can concern them very much.[3]

Massis attacks what he calls 'Eastern propagandists', an expression which is itself a contradiction in terms, since, as we have said often enough, the mania for propaganda is a purely Western thing;

3. We know that Massis is not unacquainted with our works, but he carefully avoids making the least allusion to them, since they would tell against his thesis; this procedure is, to say the least, lacking in frankness. However, such an omission is not without its advantages, as it prevents things that by their very nature should remain above discussion being dragged into distasteful polemics; there is always something distressing in profane incomprehension, even though the truth of the sacred doctrine is, in itself, too lofty to be reached by its assaults.

and this alone shows that there is some misunderstanding. In fact, among the propagandists he has in mind, we can distinguish two groups, and the first of them is exclusively composed of Westerners; to see Germans and Russians included among the representatives of the Eastern outlook would be truly ludicrous, if it were not a sign of the most deplorable ignorance of all that concerns the East; some of the observations made by the author concerning this group are very appropriate, but why does he not openly show them up for what they are? To this first group should also be added the Anglo-Saxon 'Theosophists' and the inventors of all other sects of the same kind, whose oriental terminology is no more than a mask serving to impose upon the gullible and ill-informed, and to conceal ideas no less foreign to the East than they are dear to the modern West. People of this sort are more dangerous than mere philosophers, owing to their pretensions to an esoterism they do not possess any more than do the philosophers, but which they simulate fraudulently in order to attract people who are in search of something better than 'profane' speculations and who, in the midst of the present chaos, do not know where to turn; we are surprised that Massis scarcely mentions them. As to the second group we find in it several of the Westernized Easterners to whom we referred above; such people are as ignorant of real Eastern ideas as are the first group, and they would therefore be quite incapable of spreading them in the West even should they wish to do so. As a matter of fact, the aim they really set themselves is just the opposite of this, since they wish to destroy these very ideas in the East and, at the same time, to exhibit to the West their modernized East, which has been made to conform to the theories that have been instilled in them in Europe and America. Avowed agents, as they are, of the most baneful of all forms of Western propaganda—bearing as it does directly on the intelligence—they are a danger only to the East, and not to the West, of which they are a mere reflection. Of real Easterners, Massis does not mention a single one, and he would have found it very hard to do so, for he certainly does not know any; his total inability to cite the name of any Easterner who was not Westernized should have given him cause for thought, and made him understand that 'Eastern propagandists' do not in fact exist.

Furthermore, although this compels us to speak personally, which we are not in the habit of doing, the following formal declaration is necessary: as far as we are aware, there is no one else who has expounded authentic Eastern ideas in the West; and we have always done so exactly as any Easterner would have done in the same circumstances, that is to say without the slightest intention of propaganda or popularization, and exclusively for the sake of those who are capable of understanding the doctrines as they are, without having recourse to any distortion in order to bring them within their reach; and we may add that, despite the decline of intellectuality in the West, those who understand, though obviously only a small minority, are nevertheless not so few as might have been expected. What Massis has in view are completely different undertakings—let us not say out of zeal for his cause, though the political tone of his book would justify these words; instead, in order to be as kind as possible, let us say that his mind is troubled by a fear that Western civilization is near its end, and that this has caused him to believe in the existence of 'Eastern propaganda'. At the same time, we may regret that he has been unable to discern the real causes that may indeed bring about this collapse, even though he does at times show a just severity toward certain aspects of the modern world. This is what causes the continual fluctuation in his thesis: on the one hand he is not quite sure who are the adversaries he has to fight against, and on the other his 'traditionalism' leaves him very ignorant of all that constitutes the very essence of tradition, which he obviously confuses with a sort of politico-religious conservatism of the most outward kind.

The best proof that Massis's mind is disturbed by fear is the extraordinary and completely incredible attitude he ascribes to these so-called 'Eastern propagandists'. He would have us believe that they are animated by a savage hatred of the West, and that it is only to injure the West that they are striving to impart their own doctrines to her, that is to say to bestow on her the most precious thing they possess, which constitutes, in a way, the very essence of their spirit! One is reduced to a state of bewilderment by the sheer contradictoriness of such a hypothesis: the whole laboriously erected argument crumbles in a moment, yet it would seem that the author has not even perceived this, for we are loath to suppose that he can have been aware of all the improbability of such a theory, and simply counted on his readers' lack of insight to cause them to believe it. A little elementary reflection should be enough to make it plain that the first thing for Easterners to do, if they hated the West so violently, would be to guard their doctrines jealously for their own exclusive use, and that all their efforts would be toward denying Westerners access to them; indeed, this is a reproach that has sometimes been leveled against Easterners, and with more appearance of justification. The truth, however, is rather different: the authentic representatives of the Eastern doctrines feel hatred for nobody, and there is only one reason for their reserve: it is that they consider it utterly useless to display certain truths before those who are incapable of understanding them; but they have never refused to make them known to those who possess the necessary 'qualifications', whatever may be their place of origin; is it their fault if, among such, there are very few Westerners? And, at the same time, if the mass of Easterners have come at last to be really hostile to the Westerners, after having long regarded them with indifference, whose fault is it? Must one blame the elite, who, given over to intellectual contemplation, hold themselves strictly aloof from all outward agitation, or is it not rather the fault of Westerners themselves, who have done everything to make their presence odious and intolerable? As soon as the question is put thus, as it should be, the answer becomes clear to everybody, and even if one admits that Easterners, who have hitherto given evidence of incredible patience, show at last a desire to be masters in their own home, who can bring himself honestly to blame them? It is true that, when certain passions come into play, the same things can be appreciated in a very different, and even quite contrary, sense according to the circumstances: so, for instance, when a Western people resists a foreign invasion, this is called 'patriotism' and merits the highest praise, but when an Eastern people does so it is called 'fanaticism' or 'xenophobia', and merits hatred and contempt. Moreover, is it not in the name of 'Right', and 'Liberty', of 'Justice' and 'Civilization', that the Europeans claim to impose their dominion over all others, and to forbid anyone to live and think otherwise than they do themselves? It cannot be denied that moralism is a truly remarkable thing, unless one prefers to conclude, as we do, that, save for exceptions as honorable as they are rare, there remain in the West really only two kinds of people, neither of them very interesting: the gullible, who take these big words at their face value, and believe in their 'civilizing mission', completely unaware of the materialist barbarism in which they are sunk, and the guileful, who exploit this state of mind to gratify their instincts of violence and cupidity. In any case, one thing is certain, and that is that Easterners are a menace to nobody and do not dream of invading the West in any way whatsoever: they have enough to do for the moment in defending themselves against European oppression, which threatens now to assail even their minds; and it is curious, to say the least, to see the aggressors taking up the pose of victims.

This clarification was necessary, for these are things that needed to be said; but we should consider it a waste of time to dwell at greater length on this theme, for the argument of the 'defenders of the West' is too flimsy and inconsistent. Moreover, if we have momentarily abandoned our usual attitude of reserve toward individuals in order to quote Henri Massis, it is mainly because, in the circumstances, he represents a part of the contemporary mentality, a part that must be taken into account in the present study of the state of the modern world. How can this low-grade and to a large extent artificial traditionalism, with its narrow horizons and lack of understanding, offer any real and effective resistance to an outlook, so many of whose prejudices it shares? Both outlooks imply much the same ignorance of true principles: there is the same biased denial of everything that transcends a certain limit, the same inability to understand the existence of different civilizations, and the same superstition of Greco-Latin classicism. This inadequate reaction has no other interest for us than that it shows a certain dissatisfaction with the present state of things among some of our contemporaries. There are moreover other manifestations of the same dissatisfaction, which might prove capable of going further if they were rightly guided, but for the time being all this is very chaotic, and it is still difficult to say what will come of it. Some predictions regarding this point may nevertheless be of use and, as they bear directly on the destiny of the present world, they can at the same time serve to conclude the present work, insofar as it is possible to draw conclusions without giving 'profane' ignorance an easy opening for attack by imprudently developing considerations that it would be impossible to justify in the ordinary ways. We are not one of those who think that all things can be spoken of indiscriminately, at least when one leaves pure doctrine and goes on to its applications; some reservations are necessary, and there are questions of opportuneness that cannot be overlooked. But this rightful and even indispensable reserve has nothing in common with puerile fears that are but the outcome of ignorance, comparable to the terror of the man in the Hindu proverb who 'mistakes a rope for a snake'. Whether people like it or not, what should be said will be said as circumstances dictate; neither the self-interested efforts of some people, nor the unconscious hostility of others, can prevent this, nor on the other hand will the impatience of those who are caught up by the feverish hurry of the modern world and who would like to know everything at once, cause certain things to be made known before their proper time. But the latter can at least console themselves with the thought that the ever increasing speed of events will doubtless satisfy their desires before long; may they then not come to regret having insufficiently prepared themselves to receive knowledge that they have sought more often with enthusiasm than with true discernment.

9

SOME
CONCLUSIONS

OUR CHIEF PURPOSE in this work has been to show how it is possible, by the application of traditional data, to find the most direct solution to the questions that are being asked nowadays, to explain the present state of mankind, and at the same time to judge everything that constitutes modern civilization in accordance with truth, instead of by conventional rules or sentimental preferences. We make no claim to have exhausted the subject, or to have treated it in full detail, nor to have developed all its aspects completely and without omissions. The principles that have inspired us throughout make it necessary, in any case, to present views that are essentially synthetic, and not analytical—as are those of 'profane' learning; but just because these views are synthetic, they go much further in the direction of a true explanation than could any analysis, which indeed can scarcely have more than a merely descriptive value. We think that enough has been said to enable those who are capable of understanding to deduce for themselves at least some of the consequences implicitly contained therein; and they can rest assured that the work of so doing will be of far more value to them than reading something that leaves no matter for reflection and meditation, for which latter, on the contrary, we have sought to provide an appropriate starting-point, that is to say a foundation from which to rise above the meaningless multitude of individual opinions.

It still remains to comment briefly on what might be called the practical bearing of such a study; this could be passed over or ignored if we had confined ourselves to purely metaphysical doctrine, in relation to which no application is more than contingent and accidental; but in the present study, applications are precisely the thing with which we have been concerned. These have a twofold justification quite apart from any practical value: they are the legitimate consequence of principles, the normal development of a doctrine which, since it is one and universal, must embrace all orders of reality without exception and, at the same time, as we explained when speaking of 'sacred science', these principles also form, at least for some, a preparatory means for attaining to a higher knowledge. Furthermore, while in the realm of applications, there is no harm in considering these for their own sake, provided that in so doing one is never led into losing sight of their dependence on principles. This last is a very real danger, since it is the source of the degeneracy that made 'profane science' possible, but it does not exist for those who know that everything derives from, and is altogether dependent on, pure intellectuality, and consequently that anything that does not proceed consciously therefrom can be no more than illusion. As we have said many times already, the starting-point of everything should be knowledge; and thus what appears to be most remote from the practical order is nevertheless the most potent even within this order, since it is impossible here as anywhere else to accomplish without it anything of real value or anything that will prove more than a vain and superficial agitation. But to return more particularly to the question that concerns us here, it may be said that the modern world would immediately cease to exist if men understood what it really is, since its existence, like that of ignorance and everything that implies limitation, is purely negative: it exists only through negation of the traditional and supra-human truth. Thus, through knowledge, the change could be brought about without the intervention of a catastrophe, a thing that seems scarcely possible in any other way; is it then not right to say that such knowledge can have truly incalculable practical consequences? At the same time, it is unfortunately very difficult to conceive of all men attaining to such knowledge, from which most of them are further removed than ever before; but as a matter of fact, it is quite unnecessary for them to do so, and it would be enough if there were a numerically small but powerfully established elite to guide the masses, who would obey its suggestions without even suspecting its existence, or having any idea of its mode of action; is it still possible for this elite to be effectively established in the West?

We do not intend to repeat here everything we have already said elsewhere as to the part that the intellectual elite will have to play in the various circumstances that can be regarded as possible in a not too distant future. We will confine ourself to saying this: in whatever way the change, which may be described as a passage from one world to another, may come about—whether these 'worlds' be larger or smaller cycles does not matter—it can never involve absolute discontinuity, since there is always a causal chain linking the cycles together, even though the change may have the appearance of an abrupt breach. If the elite of which we spoke could be formed while there is still time, it could so prepare the change that it would take place in the most favorable conditions possible, and the disturbances that must inevitably accompany it would in this way be reduced to a minimum; but even if this cannot be, it will still have another, and more important, task—that of contributing to the conservation of the elements that must survive from the present world to be used in forming the one to follow. One knows that a re-ascent must come, but it is nevertheless unnecessary to wait for the descent to reach its nadir before preparing the way for the re-ascent, even though it may prove impossible to prevent the descent ending in some cataclysm beforehand. This means that, whatever may happen, the work done will not be wasted: it cannot be useless, if only because of the benefit that the elite itself will draw from it, but neither will it be wasted from the point of view of its later effects on humanity as a whole.

Here then is how things may be envisaged: the elite still exists in the Eastern civilizations, and, granting that it is becoming ever smaller due to modernist encroachment, it will nevertheless continue to exist until the end, because this is necessary for the safeguarding of the 'ark' of tradition—which cannot perish—and for the transmission of everything that is to be preserved. In the West on the other hand the elite no longer exists; the question may therefore be asked whether or not it will be reconstituted before the end of our epoch, that is, whether the Western world, despite its deviation, will take part in this work of preservation and transmission. If not, the result will be that Western civilization will have to disappear completely, since, having lost all trace of the traditional spirit, it will no longer contain any element that is of use for the future. The question, thus posed, may have only a very secondary importance as far as the final result is concerned; it nevertheless has, from a relative point of view, a certain interest that cannot be overlooked, once we decide to take into consideration the particular conditions of the times in which we live. In principle, it would be sufficient to note that this Western world is a part of the whole from which it appears to have become separated at the beginning of the modern era, and that all parts must to a certain extent contribute toward the ultimate reintegration of the cycle. But this does not necessarily imply any prior restoration of the Western tradition, since the latter may be preserved only in a state of permanent possibility at its source, and not in any particular form that it may have assumed at a given period. We merely mention this in passing, for in order to make it fully understandable it would be necessary to examine in detail the relationship between the primordial tradition and the subordinate traditions, and this we cannot do here. In itself, this would be the most unfavorable outcome for the Western world, but the present state of things in the West gives rise to the fear that it is the one that is actually being realized; however, as we have said, there are some signs that seem to show that all hope of a better solution need not yet be entirely abandoned.

There are at present more people in the West than one might suppose who are beginning to see what is wanting in their civilization; if they fall back on vague aspirations and embark on research that is often barren, and if they sometimes even lose their way altogether, it is because they lack real knowledge, which nothing can replace, and because there is no organization that can give them the doctrinal guidance they need. We do not refer here, of course, to those who have succeeded in finding such guidance in the Eastern traditions and who are therefore, intellectually, outside the Western world; such persons must necessarily remain exceptional cases, and cannot in any way form an integral part of a Western elite; they are in reality a prolongation of the Eastern elites and might form a link between these and that of the West, once this be established; but a

Western elite can by definition only be established by Western initiative, and therein lies the whole difficulty. This initiative could come in one of two ways: either the West would have to find in itself the means of bringing it about through a direct return to its own tradition, a return that would be a sort of spontaneous reawakening of latent possibilities; or certain Western elements would have to bring about this restoration with the help afforded by a knowledge of the Eastern doctrines; this however could not for them be quite direct, since they would have to remain Westerners, but it might be obtained by a sort of second-hand influence working through intermediaries such as those of whom we have just spoken. The first of these two hypotheses is very unlikely, since it depends on the existence in the West of at least one rallying point where the traditional spirit has been preserved intact, and as we have already said, this seems to us very doubtful, notwithstanding certain affirmations to the contrary; it is therefore the second hypothesis that needs to be examined more closely.

In this case it would be better, although not absolutely necessary, for the elite to be able to take as its basis a Western organization already enjoying an effective existence. It seems quite clear that there is now but one organization in the West that is of a traditional character and that has preserved a doctrine that could serve as an appropriate basis for the work in question, and this organization is the Catholic church. It would be enough to restore to the doctrine of the Church, without changing anything of the religious form that it bears outwardly, the deeper meaning that is truly contained in it, but of which its present representatives seem to be unaware, just as they are unaware of its essential unity with the other traditional forms—these two things being, as a matter of fact, inseparable from one another. This would mean the realization of Catholicism in the true sense of the word, which etymologically expresses the idea of 'universality', a fact that is too apt to be forgotten by those who seek to make of it no more than the denomination of one particular and purely Western form, without any real connection with the other traditions. Indeed, it may be said that in the present state of things Catholicism has no more than a virtual existence, since it does not possess any real awareness of universality; but it is nonetheless true that the existence of an organization bearing such a name is in itself an indication that there is a possible basis for a restoration of the traditional spirit in its fullest sense, the more so because throughout the Middle Ages it already served as a support for it in the West. All that would be necessary therefore is to re-establish what already existed prior to the modern deviation, though with the adaptations called for by the conditions of a different period; and if such an idea astonishes or offends some people, it is because they themselves, though unconsciously and perhaps even against their will, are so completely governed by the modern outlook as to have quite forgotten the meaning of a tradition of which they retain only the outer shell. The important question is whether the formalism of the 'letter'—this being also a variety of materialism as we have defined it earlier on—has utterly smothered spirituality or only temporarily overshadowed it, leaving the possibility of a re-awakening within the existing organization; only the course of events can give an answer to this question.

It is possible that this same course of events might sooner or later force on the leaders of the Catholic church, as an unavoidable necessity, a decision whose intellectual import they would be far from properly understanding. It would certainly be a matter for regret if they should be driven to reflection by circumstances as contingent as those springing from the field of politics, at least as long as this is considered apart from any higher principle. But at the same time, it must be admitted that the opportunity for the development of latent possibilities must be accorded to each person through those means that most immediately fall within the scope of his present understanding. For this reason, we do not hesitate to assert, in view of the ever increasing state of confusion, that it has become necessary to call for the union of all the spiritual forces whose action still makes itself felt in the outer world, in both the West and the East; and as far as the West is concerned, we can see no other such force than the Catholic church. If the latter could thus be brought into touch with representatives of the Eastern traditions, it would be a preliminary step, at which we would rejoice, being possibly the starting-point for what we have in mind, inasmuch as it would doubtless not be long before it became apparent that a merely outward and 'diplomatic' understanding was illusory, and could not yield the desired results; it would then become necessary to pass on to what would normally come first, namely to consider a possible agreement on principles. For this agreement, the one and only essential condition is for the representatives of the West to return to a real awareness of those principles, which the East has never lost. A true mutual understanding, be it said once more, can come only from above and within, which means that it must be in the domain that can be called, with equal truth, intellectual or spiritual, since the two words really bear the same meaning. From this starting-point, the understanding would be bound to extend over all other domains, just as, once a principle is enunciated, it only remains to extract—or rather to make more explicit—all the consequences implied therein. There can only be one obstacle in the way of such an understanding, and that is Western proselytism, which cannot bring itself to admit that it is sometimes necessary to have 'allies' who are not 'subjects'; to put it more correctly, the obstacle is the lack of understanding, of which this proselytism is only one of the products. Can this obstacle be overcome? If not, the elite, in establishing itself, would be able to count only on the efforts of those who were qualified by their intellectual capacity, apart from any particular environment, and also, of course, on the support of the East; its work would thereby be made more difficult, and its influence could only make itself felt after a longer interval, as it would itself have to create all the necessary instruments, instead of finding them ready to hand, as in the other case; but we are far from supposing that these difficulties, however great they may be, are of a kind that could in any way prevent the work that has to be done.

We therefore consider it opportune to make the following statement: there are already, in the Western world, signs of a movement that is still ill-defined but that may—and even, if things take their normal course, must—lead to the re-establishment of an intellectual elite, unless a cataclysm comes too quickly for it to have had time to develop fully. It is scarcely necessary to say that the Church would have every interest, as far as the part to be played by it in the future is concerned, in giving its support to such a movement rather than letting it take place independently and being obliged later to follow it in order to retain an influence that threatened to disappear. It is not necessary to adopt a particularly lofty or difficult point of view to see that it is the Church that would benefit the most by an attitude which, far from involving the slightest compromise in the field of doctrine, would in fact have the contrary result of freeing it from all infiltration of the modern spirit, and which at the same time would entail no outward changes. It would be something of a paradox to see integral Catholicism realized without the collaboration of the Catholic church, which might find itself under the strange necessity of submitting to being defended against onslaughts more terrible than any it has yet faced by men whom its leaders, or at any rate those whom they allow to speak in their name, had at first tried to discredit by casting on them the most ill-founded suspicions. For our own part, we would be sorry to see this happen; but if it is not to come to this, it is high time for those whose position places on them grave responsibilities to act with open eyes on the matters at issue, and no longer allow attempts, which might have consequences of the utmost importance, to run the danger of frustration owing to the incomprehension or ill-will of certain more or less subordinate individuals—a thing that has happened before now, and is one more sign of the extent to which confusion reigns everywhere today. We shall doubtless receive no gratitude for this warning, which is given quite independently and disinterestedly; but this is of no importance, and we shall continue nonetheless to say what has to be said, whenever it becomes necessary, and in the form that we consider most suited to the circumstances. The foregoing is only a summary of the conclusions to which we have been led by recent investigations, carried out, it is scarcely necessary to add, in a purely intellectual field. There is no need, at least for the moment, to give a detailed description of them, and indeed this could have little interest in itself; but it may be affirmed that not a single word of what has been said above has been written without ample reflection. It should be clearly understood that it would be utterly useless to put forward here, by way of objection, any more or less specious philosophical arguments; we are speaking seriously, of serious matters, and have no time to waste on verbal disputes that would be of no interest, and could serve no useful purpose. Moreover, it is our intention to remain entirely aloof from all controversies and quarrels of school or party, just as we refuse absolutely to accept any Western label or definition, since none is applicable; whether this is pleasing or displeasing, it is a fact, and nothing will change our attitude in this regard.

A warning must be addressed to those who, because of their capacity for a higher understanding, if not because of the degree of knowledge to which they have actually attained, seem destined to become elements of a possible elite. There is no doubt that the force of modernism, which is truly 'diabolic' in every sense of the word, strives by every means in its power to prevent these elements, today isolated and scattered, from achieving the cohesion that is necessary if they are to exert any real influence on the general mentality. It is therefore for those who have already more or less completely become aware of the end toward which their efforts should be directed to stand firm against whatever difficulties may arise in their path and threaten to turn them aside. Those who have not yet reached the point beyond which an infallible guidance makes it henceforth impossible to stray from the true path always remain in danger of the most serious deviations; they need to display the utmost prudence; we would even say that prudence should be carried to the point of distrust, for the 'adversary', who up to this point has not yet been definitively overcome, can assume the most varied, and at times the most unexpected, disguises. It can happen that those who think they have escaped from modern materialism fall a prey to things that, while seemingly opposed to it, are really of the same order; and, in view of the turn of mind of modern Westerners, a special warning needs to be uttered against the attraction that more or less extraordinary phenomena may hold for them; it is this attraction that is to a large extent responsible for all the errors of 'neo-spiritualism', and it is to be foreseen that the dangers it represents will grow even worse, for the forces of darkness, which keep alive the present confusion, find in it one of their most potent instruments. It is even probable that we are not very far from the time referred to by the prophecy of the Gospel to which we have already alluded elsewhere: 'For false Christs and false prophets shall arise, and shall show signs and wonders to seduce, if it were possible, even the elect.' The 'elect' (the 'chosen') are the elite in the fullness of its meaning, according to the sense in which we have invariably used the word: those who, by virtue of the inner 'realization' they have achieved, can no longer be seduced; but this is not the case with those who, as yet, possess only the possibilities of knowledge, and who are therefore, properly speaking, only the 'called'; and this is why the Gospels say that 'many are called, but few are chosen.' We are entering upon a period when it will be extremely difficult to 'separate the grain from the chaff' and carry out effectively what theologians call the 'discerning of spirits', both because of the general confusion manifesting itself in intensified and ever more varied forms, and also because of the want of true knowledge on the part of those whose normal function should be to guide the rest, but who today only too often are no more than 'blind guides'. We shall see whether the subtleties of dialectic are of any avail in such circumstances, and whether any philosophy, even were it the best possible, can have the strength to prevent the 'infernal powers' from being let loose; this also is an illusion against which some people need to guard, for it is too often supposed, in ignorance of what pure intellectuality really is, that a merely philosophical knowledge, which even in the best of cases is a bare shadow of true knowledge, can put everything to rights and turn the contemporary mentality away from its deviation; in the same way, there are those who think they can find in modern science itself a means of raising themselves to the higher truths, whereas this science is in fact founded on the negation of those truths. All these illusions are so many influences leading people astray, and by their means many who sincerely desire to react against the modern outlook are reduced to impotence, since, having failed to find the essential principles without which all action is in vain, they have been swept into blind alleys from which there is no escape.

Those who will succeed in overcoming all these obstacles, and triumphing over the hostility of an environment opposed to all spirituality, will doubtless be few in number; but let it be said once more that it is not numbers that count, for we are here in a domain whose laws are quite different from those of matter. There is therefore no cause for despair, and, even were there no hope of achieving any visible result before the modern world collapses under some catastrophe, this would still be no valid reason for not undertaking a work whose scope extends far beyond the present time. Those who might be tempted to give way to despair should realize that nothing accomplished in this order can ever be lost, that confusion, error, and darkness can win the day only in appearance and in a purely ephemeral way, that all partial and transitory disequilibriums must perforce contribute toward the greater equilibrium of the whole, and that nothing can ultimately prevail against the power of truth; their motto should be the one formerly used by certain initiatic organizations of the West: *Vincit omnia Veritas.*

INDEX

Made in the
USA
Middletown, DE